Introduction to Home Economics

Books by Mrs. White

Mother's Faith

For the Love of Christian Homemaking

Early Morning Revival Challenge

Mother's Book of Home Economics

Living on His Income

Old Fashioned Motherhood

Economy for the Christian Home

Mother's Hour

At Mother's House

Introduction to Home Economics

Cover Photo: Table in Mrs. White's home.
Back Cover: He ing table in the parlour.

Introduction to Home nomics

Introduction to Home Economics

Gentle Instruction to Find Joy in Christian Homemaking

The Legacy of Home Press
puritanlight@gmail.com

Introduction to Home Economics
Copyright 2018 by Mrs. Sharon White
All Rights Reserved

The Legacy of Home Press
ISBN-13: 978-0692189177
ISBN-10: 0692189173
Introduction to Home Economics: Gentle Instruction to Find Joy in Christian Homemaking
Author – Mrs. Sharon White

Contents

Introduction

Whether you are currently a homemaker or want training in your future vocation at home, this course will provide a peaceful and pleasant study. The chapters are like visits over tea at my Vermont home. These include articles, memories, and encouragement to be a joyful homemaker in a godly home.

You could simply read through the book at your own pace. There are 24 chapters per unit. By reading 6 of the short chapters each week, a unit can be completed in about a month.

There are 3 units with subjects covering life and lessons on:

"Family and Home;" "New England Thrift;" and, "To Be a Lady."

You will find a section for questions and space provided for a "homemaker's diary."

There are three projects to complete along with each unit. These cover the most important aspects of work for the mother at home. To manage money well, keep a clean home, and prepare nourishing food is essential to a happy home. You will learn:

1) How to keep a financial record for the home by setting up a "House Account."

2) How to set up a simple menu plan.

3) How to do a cleaning challenge.

The foundation of the course is found in essays of instruction and encouragement, through reading about the daily life of a New England Homemaker.

Unit One

Family and Home

{Photograph on previous page: A Room in Mrs. White's Home}

1

Pretending to Garden

It is supposed to rain for the next several days. I keep trying to get outside and do some gardening. I am only an amateur so I don't do very much. Late this afternoon, I put on my gardening gloves and went up to the back property by the river. This is where our strawberry garden rests, right beside a nice bench for me to sit and take my breaks.

When I finished a few sections, I started to walk the property. I take my time, stopping to look at many of the trees. Today, I saw some wild daisies growing by the side fence. I was delighted!

I also saw tiny little blue flowers, yellow ones, and white ones. I have no idea what kind they are, but they are probably weeds. They grow, here and there, throughout our two acres.

When I am walking the grounds, in late afternoon, I often see three of my grandbabies standing in the front picture window. They are so excited to see me outside! Soon their Mother brings them out and we all have a lovely time in the front yard. The children love picking flowers and weeds, just for fun. They will pick two tiny flowers and give one to *Mother* and one to *Grandmother*. They laugh and run and enjoy the Estate so much! It is a delight to sit and watch them in their happiness.

Sometimes, the children wonder what I am doing on my walks.

They see me staring at the different leaves on the many trees, looking for changes, and enjoying the beauty of nature. As I walk along the property, I hear birds singing and hear the beautiful sound of the rushing river at the edge of our Estate. This, I suppose, is what is called a "nature walk."

I have no idea what I am doing, or what I am seeing. I will often pull up some random weeds, here and there. Or, I will pull off dead leaves from a plant or tree. I call this, "pretending to garden."

This is how I am learning, by just walking around, observing, and trying to garden. It is a peaceful work. It is a cheerful pastime. This is also how we learn to keep house, be a good wife, and to mother our dear children. We just play at it, we pretend, we have fun with it, and this gives us the knowledge and experience, *over time*, to do it well.

2

The Duty of Housekeeping

I had to tell Papa, in the nicest way possible, to get out of my kitchen. I would catch him doing the dishes, cleaning the counters, and picking up the children's toys. He was doing it to help me. He wanted me to rest. He thought I had too much to do. "But," I told him. "You are doing *my* work." I did not want to be idle. To me, there is a great difference between laziness and necessary rest. If I do not have my usual work to do, I would feel lazy. This would cause me to put on weight from lack of activity. This would take away my joy of being the housekeeper.

Papa had his own things to do, like walking, and trying to continue his recovery (from a disabling accident a few years ago). He also had little projects he could work on in the garage.   When he was doing my work, I would hear him sigh. This was because he was in pain. He was suffering from his disability but trying to work through it because he loved me. I told him that he found no happiness in housework, but I loved it. The work is part of what keeps me happy.

It started to become amusing, his helping me all the time when I didn't want help. Some of the grandchildren would be up here for breakfast and playing. Then I would walk them back downstairs, with their Mother, to their section of the house. But before I would go, I would say to Papa, "Leave the mess for me, please." As soon as I started to walk away, I would see him starting to pick up the blocks or clear the table of breakfast dishes. He would head right over to the DVD player and shut off whatever program some of the children had been watching in another room. It almost became a race as to who would clean first. It seemed like he would never even give me a chance to do anything around the house. "Papa," I would say, "Please just let me do my own work. I will be right back upstairs and will clean it all up."

It took several weeks for us to work this out. I am now able to enjoy plenty of housework. I am delighting in the work. It is my duty and I am proud to do it each day.

Yesterday, I cleaned the kitchen several times, did laundry, made homemade pizza, cake, and took care of the grandbabies. In the late afternoon, Papa saw me setting up the dishes to do some more work. He asked, "Where do you find the energy?" I told him I was very tired, but I had the will to work. That was the key. I had a strong will to do my duty of being a housekeeper and this is what gave me great joy.

3

Cheering Up Dreary Days

There are depressing days in early spring. I look out the window and see rain falling on an unpleasant sight. It is mud season. The pile – up of last winter's snow is melting, exposing muddy leaves from last fall. It is our neglected property at its worst. Some of us tried, late last fall, to rake up all the leaves on our 2 acres. But it was overwhelming. I am hoping I can organize some of the family to help me clean it up as soon as the muddy days are gone. If we can do it before the sun starts shining, before the grass and flowers start growing, our property will be pretty again for the coming season.

Still, right now, my only view out the Estate window is a terrible, dreary sight. I have to work harder to make the indoors look extra cheerful. I opened all the blinds and curtains to get a bit of faint sunshine through the clouds. I lay out as many fake flowers in pretty vases as I can. I straighten pillows on the parlour sofa, make the table and chairs look tidy, and shine and scrub to make it all pleasant.

I have to find a way to keep myself happy and create an atmosphere of joy and contentment. The grandchildren were feeling the gloominess of our surroundings. To settle them down, I turned on a lovely CD called "Christmas with Nat, Dean, and Bing." The songs were so sweet and soothing. It only takes little efforts to cheer us along through those dark days. The beauty of spring and the warmth of the coming sunshine will be worth the wait!

4

Use Your Strength Wisely

We only have so much energy to get through a day. It is important to conserve our strength and pace ourselves. We have children to take care of and homes to care for. We also have errands and grocery shopping to do. If you add teaching, in a homeschool, and making food from scratch, it can get overwhelming. Organizing our time will help keep us steady and rested.

When my children were little, we did our grocery shopping and errands on Friday mornings. There was no heavy cleaning or baking on that day. We also went to the library just before we bought our groceries. After we made it back home, and everything was put away, a simple lunch was made while all the children happily sat to read with their piles of books. It was a busy morning, but a quiet afternoon.

There are days when doing errands is so overwhelming that I avoid doing much housework when I get home. These are days to make simple meals that take little work. It is not the kind of day to do all the laundry or to vacuum all the floors. It is enough that errands were accomplished.

On other days, I will bake and clean and cook. These are staying home days. This is time to focus on baking cookies, making a special dinner, and for preparing some good food for the freezer. I have the most energy in the early morning hours, so that is when I do most of my work. In the afternoon, I will walk the property and then do quiet, restful work, with many breaks.

It is not possible to work hard at every hour throughout the day and night. That would be dangerous and would destroy our health. We have to learn to conserve our energy and to pace ourselves. That old saying about being "slow and steady" is a wonderful motto for the homemaker.

5

Mother's Home Bakery

Sometime in the middle of this month, an illness went through the house. Just as I was beginning to recover, I saw a sadness in the eyes of the men in my family (my husband and grown son). I had not been able to do much grocery shopping. The boys had been mostly left to themselves to make meals. One afternoon, I heard them say they were going to run out to the store to get something for dinner. They looked weary and in need of comfort. I realized I had not done a very good job the last few weeks in providing for the needs of the kitchen.

As soon as I was completely well, I did the month's shopping. This included the special foods required for our Chanukah and Christmas menus. I bought plenty of flour and eggs and baking supplies. I knew my boys needed to be taken care of with good homemade food.

With my energy back, I set about to bake or cook something each day. I baked the Christmas cookies and fudge. We had special treats ready for each of our 8 nights of Chanukah. Soon it was time for the turkey dinner with freshly made buttermilk biscuits on Christmas day. The baking continued the next week as I made Challah bread for the Sabbath. (This is a favorite with all my children.) Soon there were chocolate chip cookies and brownies.

One morning I thought I would make a batch of homemade donuts, using a plain recipe from my old Betty Crocker cookbook. I had never done this before and did not have a donut cutter. So, I used a snowflake - shaped cookie cutter. I lined a tray with wax paper and cut out stacks of dough to prepare for the work. Soon donuts were frying in oil and then placed on a paper towel. These were stored in a large container lined with wax paper and sprinkled with powdered sugar. What a treat for the whole family to have freshly made donuts that morning! The snowflake shape made them look extra special.

My freezer is full of a week's supply of homemade pizza made with a whole wheat crust. Papa helps me a great deal with making dinners, so I mostly do the baking. This morning I will make a batch of brownies and a pot of homemade soup. These are perfect foods for such a cold day (it is well below zero outside right now). Tomorrow I will bake an apple pie.

I love to see my boys walking in the kitchen to see what I am making. The sadness in their eyes has been replaced with happiness. They look relieved and content. They look like they love home again and have no need of running out to the store every time they are hungry.

6

A Routine for Mother

I get so distracted sometimes that I forget to eat. All of a sudden, I get weary and weak and then realize it is because I missed lunch. It is not often I get hungry, so weakness reminds me that I need nourishment. I had to make a schedule, or a routine, for myself.

These days, I always set my alarm for 6 a.m. so I can exercise and get dressed and ready for the day before anyone needs me. (If my children were babies, I would not do this! One must sleep when one can when there are small children who need constant attention.) Then at 7 a.m. I have tea.

I had to put down what time to eat breakfast, lunch, and dinner. I had to write down the different food I normally eat, so I would not get distracted or forgetful. For example, I had to write that I needed a protein shake with an apple at 11 a.m. Otherwise I might forget to include it in my day. I consider that shake to be my vitamins and main protein and it helps keep me healthy. I have been doing this, generally speaking, for 20 years.

Why do I need to write down a routine for myself? When my children were all young, it was easy to make all the meals and sit down together to eat them. It was easy to remember to eat. But when it is just me and my husband, it is not always easy to remember. His routine, or schedule, is different than mine because of his disability. He might be awake in the evening when I am asleep. Or, very often he sleeps through the breakfast hour, while I have been up for several hours.

While I don't follow the schedule exactly, it has helped me to stay on track. It has become an essential guide for my day. The schedule also reminds me that, no matter what is going on, I need to keep to a certain bedtime. I know I need to rest but would forget that too if it were not part of my routine!

Many times, I have gone out the door with one of my grown sons to do an errand or grocery shop at an odd time of day. It is not until later I realize I have forgotten to eat. With my routine written out on paper, I can avoid this, by scheduling any trips around my routine. It is similar to having a baby in the house. We don't take the baby out at his naptime and we certainly wouldn't take him out when he is supposed to eat.

If only we Mothers would take the time and care of ourselves that we need, we would feel so much better. We ought to take care of ourselves the way we take care of our little ones. This means a structured, old time routine, as was common in homes of past generations. We should not be leaving our day to whims or impulse. An orderly day, as best as we can follow, brings peace and gentleness to one's life. This will give us rest and good health.

7

All Dressed up to Keep House

One of the nicest things we can do to make home a happy place is to get dressed up. It was common for housewives to put on a pretty "house" dress and a nice apron each morning. The work of vacuuming, polishing furniture, and straightening drapes is much more fun to do when one looks pretty and has a pleasant attitude.

I have a lilac - scented candle that sets a nice mood during the day for when I am cleaning or cooking. Somehow, those little extra efforts of making the house look nice, and making oneself look extra pretty, brings a cheerfulness to the home.

Right now it is considered "mud season" here in rural Vermont. When it is not very pretty outside, it can get us feeling down. It is so important to take some time to make the indoors look inviting and cared - about. If we take the time to brighten our appearance and the appearance of our homes, it will help prevent those depressing feelings we can get when there isn't enough fresh air and sunshine.

8

Walking in the Gardens

Yesterday I picked several strawberries from the back gardens. As a new gardener, I am always amazed that I am able to get fresh strawberries, year after year, with very little work. This year, I am getting more berries than ever. It is because of Papa.

For the past few summers, I would walk across the grounds and head towards the back property. Almost every day, the birds would see me coming and quickly fly away from the strawberries they were eating! I would say, "Did you leave any for me today?" But they never answered. I just assumed I would have to share the harvest with the birds. I didn't really mind because I loved to hear them sing all spring, summer, and fall. Their chirping made me so happy.

This spring, I mentioned sharing the strawberries with the birds to Papa. He told me that, in his childhood home, his Mother always had pinwheels in her gardens. So, I bought some little cheap ones at the store. They look so pretty as the wind blows them. There is also a bright glare on them from the sun. Apparently, this is what is keeping the birds out of the gardens. I still hear the birds singing happily all over the property, but they stay out of the strawberries. I have been delighted with the large harvest I have been getting this summer!

9

Christmas Baking

It has been snowing steadily for days here in rural Vermont. It is so pretty, especially this time of year. The temperature outside was 10 degrees yesterday when I ventured out for an errand. Inside, it is cozy and pleasant by the fire.

I just made a batch of sugar cookie dough. I wrapped it in wax paper and placed it in a bowl to cool in the refrigerator. I will make the cookies much later today. I have bell - shaped cookie cutters, which are my favorite. I have red and green sugar sprinkles to decorate with.

I am just about to make Christmas fudge. It is just plain chocolate fudge made using a recipe on the label of Carnation Evaporated milk. It doesn't take long, but it requires standing by the stove and working quickly before pouring into a pan to cool. I have to make sure no one calls me on the phone, or walks in for a visit, or else I will lose my concentration. Everyone has to be settled before Mother makes the fudge.

I am just doing a few, basic things to bring cheer to the family. I don't have the energy to do anything time consuming or elaborate.

I have some pretty rose-colored carnations in a jar on my sideboard table. This sits on a red table runner. It looks festive.

I have a couple of presents, for some of the grandchildren, sitting on the floor near my rocking chair in the parlour. When the children come upstairs to visit me later today, I will let them "find" these gifts. I will smile and tell them, "*Oh, well you may as well open them, of course.*" They will be so happy! It is just warm, new pajamas for each of them.

Some of the children and grandchildren will visit over the Christmas vacation. I have a small present for each grandbaby. No matter how cold it gets, or how grumpy and tired some of us can be, we hope to attend the Christmas service at church.

I am busy sewing a couple of aprons and doing some crocheting, which keeps me busy while I sit on the parlour couch and visit with the family.

If Mother is happy and cheerful, the family cannot help but cheer up and smile too! Besides, our happiness is not based on anyone else's mood or troubles. It is based on the joyful peace we have as a child of God.

10

The Church Committee Meeting

I made a terrible mistake. I signed up to be part of a committee at our church, thinking it would only take a few minutes, now and then, after Sunday service. I had never joined any such thing, but the group was organized to create a church cookbook so I wanted to help. Everything started out just fine. It was a few minutes here and there to vote and organize ideas. But as the deadline for the publication got closer, a special meeting was called for a Friday evening.

I really thought I needed to be there. The mistake was that I left behind family at a time of day when they needed me most. There was my disabled husband, two grown children, and two grandbabies who were just finishing their dinner when I left. I felt terrible for going.

At the meeting, there were far more members present than necessary. There were a couple of questions that were quickly answered and it was over. Many lingered to talk and visit for a few minutes. By the time I got home, I had missed the grandchildren's bedtime routine. I had to clean up all the dinner mess when the house should have been quiet for those who were sleeping. I felt like I had made a serious error and had abandoned my station at home. I was not happy and did not feel at peace.

As I later thought about it, I realized I did not have to attend that evening meeting. Most of the ladies came to the brief Sunday sessions as they were able. This was an important lesson for me. I can only help if it does not take away from the needs of my own family. This is what will bring me the greatest joy and blessing.

11

The Children's Cookbook

I love when the grandchildren are here to help with my chores and baking. My 4 – year old granddaughter is the first one to notice if there are dishes that need to be washed. She sets up two stools by the sink – one for me and one for her. She says, "*Me`me, it's time to do the dishes.*" I wash the plates, bowls, cups, and silverware, handing each item to her to put in the drainer. We work together to get everything cleaned up.

One afternoon, grand-girl was sitting at the parlour table with me. She glanced toward the kitchen and noticed a stack of clean dishes in the drainer. She asked, "*Who did the dishes.*" I smiled and said, "*I did them.*" She looked surprised and said, "*All by yourself?*"

Most mornings I am baking muffins or brownies and the children sit right nearby and watch as I do the work. One day, my 5-year old grandson decided to make a cookbook. He drew pictures and letters on each page. There were brownies and spaghetti and all kinds of things. He is still learning to read and write so his words look so cute and I often need him to help me to read it all. His homemade cookbook is adorable.

On the last page of the book is a prayer. He had drawn a picture and written out (to the best of his ability) the prayer I taught him to say before meals. I had never heard of a cookbook with prayers and thought he was so clever and sweet! I love that the children say their prayers with me at our kitchen table. We even say prayers when we have snacks. I think every cookbook ought to have "grace" or a prayer printed out for us to say before we eat.

The children's cookbook is just a bunch of plain paper, folded over, and stapled down the center. Grandson colored it and created it all on his own. One afternoon, just before I started to make a cake- batter, he brought in his book and said, "*Here, Me`me. You need the cookbook*." I set it up by the mixing bowl to the "brownie" page and got right to work. He was delighted!

12

Chore Cards for Mother

When my children were little, they did a great deal of housework. We had lists of chores, assigned work, and chores written out on index cards. There was always someone around to do the daily and weekly duties.

I am finding myself alone in housekeeping these days, since my children are all adults now. It is overwhelming to maintain our large house on my own. But I will admit that I am sidetracked and forgetful in my older years!

My solution is to make myself chore cards, just like I used to make for my children. I will sit at the kitchen table and write one chore on each card. These will be simple things like "sweep the hallway" or "wash the bedroom windows." I will also write out harder work like "wash the kitchen floor." I think I will use white cards for easy chores and colored cards for harder ones. This way, depending on how much energy I have, I can at least quickly choose a chore based on the color of the card.

I don't expect my house to be showroom clean because I simply do not have the strength to do this all myself. But at least each and every day, I can pick up a couple of the cards and get some of this work done. Over the course of days and weeks, things will be much cleaner around here!

13

Taking Care of the Home

We had a couple of large trees removed from the property this month. They were dangerously close to our house and became a hazard. This has left quite a bit of work for us to do. There is much firewood to cut and stack. The boys use a wheelbarrow to haul stacks of it to the garage, where pieces are then cut to a suitable size for the wood stove. Since the trees are gone, there is a clear view of a side of our house that I have never really seen. It is in desperate need of paint and makes our home look even more shabby than before.

To take care of the grounds, to maintain the house, and to keep things clean and orderly indoors is a tremendous amount of work. But work is good for us and helps keep us healthy.

Indoors, I have been cleaning and organizing my dressing room. Old files and papers are being discarded. Bags are being filled up with books I no longer need. Bookcases are being straightened and made neat again. It is starting to look better but will always be a regular task to keep the house in order.

While I was working the other day, the grandchildren came to visit me. I had stacks of things all over the floor. I was delighted to have them help me. Then it was time for a rest. I had several tea breaks with different members of the family throughout the day.

In the midst of the maintenance work, there are still the daily duties of laundry, cooking, baking, and cleaning the kitchen. Pacing myself will always be a challenge. I tend to do far more than I should without taking enough breaks. This is something I am trying to improve.

Years ago, I remember my mother-in-law visiting us from Massachusetts. She was an excellent housewife and homemaker, and an incredible example to me. She saw our old house and the many rooms and wondered how I would ever keep up with the work. I wonder that too sometimes!

The weather has been unusually warm. I walked the property with Mister in the late afternoon yesterday. We sat on the bench, back by the river, beside my strawberry garden. It is nice to take breaks.

I have plenty of work today to keep me busy and happy. We will also have company at different times of the day, which will be wonderful.

14

Doing Good Things

There are people who find happiness in coming to a complete stop at traffic lights and stop signs, even if there are no other cars around. They look both ways, count a few seconds, and then go when it is safe. They do this with a happy feeling of goodness, even when they are alone.

It is precious to do good things, to act in good ways, and to follow rules of order, etiquette, and kindness. This makes us happy.

Early this month, I went to the hospital every day. A little baby had been born to my oldest son and his fiancé. She does not have much family in the area, so I checked on her each day to see what she needed. I helped her with paperwork, encouraged her to rest, and helped get the car- seat in place for when they could go home.

I told her that I would bring her a hot supper her first night at home. Hospitals do such a good job bringing you three nice meals a day. When you get back home, you miss someone else making nutritious food for you. She needed to focus on resting and caring for her new baby.

Bringing a hot meal to someone is what grandmothers do. It is often what churches organize for those in need. I realized it was going to take extra work and driving for me, but it was a gesture that would make her more comfortable and less stressed her first night home. Many new mothers, these modern days, are so neglected and are expected to do too much on their own. We older ones ought to take on the extra work to bring cheer and happiness to them.

In the afternoon of her release date, I made a big batch of lasagna. A large portion was placed in each of 2 portable aluminum foil pans. There were flat covers on them with room to write what the pans contained. I also packed bakery Italian bread, buttered with parmesan cheese. I made 2 tiny salads as a side dish and packed them in plastic containers.

Next, I prepared a treat for the following morning's breakfast. I put freshly cut cantaloupe in plastic containers. Then I packed homemade oatmeal- peanut butter-chocolate chip muffins, I had baked earlier in the day. This "breakfast" went into lunch bags.

As soon as everything was ready, I drove over to their house and delivered the special food. The new mother was delighted!

I was exhausted.

But it was such a happy time. These are the special labors that create memories of a loving family. There are occasions for birthdays, Thanksgiving, holidays, birth, and events where we can work hard to bring joy to others by taking care of them. It is a way of mothering them and wanting them to be happy and encouraged through our efforts. It is a blessing for all of us when we make it a habit to do good things.

15

The First Housekeeping Day of the Year

The other night, I cleaned our kitchen and parlour before I went to sleep. I wanted it to look nice because that makes me happy. I want to reflect a little on this since it is the first day of the New Year.

No matter how tired I am, I try to make the effort of having the main rooms of the house put "to rights" before I rest. This often takes herculean courage and an incredible attitude of "with a will."

I am not young, nor am I old. But life has taken its toll on me. I get worn out incredibly easily. I do rest when I must, but I have to get back to the duties of homemaking to accomplish lovely things here for my family.

The lovely things of home, for me, are just keeping things simple and peaceful. It is peaceful to have homemade meals made on a daily basis. This keeps us nourished with wholesome food. It is peaceful to fluff pillows and straiten the couch cover in the parlour. I want the couch and chairs to look inviting so people can take the time of rest and refreshment here before getting back to their daily work.

I have grown children, a teenager, toddlers, and babies here on a daily basis. They play, eat, run around, and enjoy home. They do not make "messes," they simply "live." I clean up as we go, or when they are finished. They are my helpers as we often do chores together. I feel blessed as I work as I am so grateful to have them all here. It is a privilege to be the wife, mother, and grandmother of a family.

Sometimes, if I am terribly worn out, I will leave the crayons on the kitchen table. I will leave my tea cup there as well. I will leave the papers, and the cups from the children's juice. I will leave the chairs out from the morning activity. I am greatly amused when, later in the day, a little grandchild will come back to visit me, glance at the table, and looking worried, say, "Me`me didn't clean up the mess?" It is funny because he knows how much I love to clean and he thought something was wrong with his beloved grandmother! This sweet little comment gave me the energy to get it all tidied up with his help.

We cannot have perfectly spotless houses in showroom condition. Certainly not. But we can take the time, throughout the day, to be about the business of housekeeping. It takes work and effort and creativity to keep a home in order. It also takes a cheerful willingness to make home a peaceful, happy place to be.

The nice thing about being a good homemaker is we don't have to wait for a New Year to start. We can start fresh every morning.

16

Running from Home

For the past few months, since we have guests staying here for a long visit, I have been running around quite a bit. We do errands, visiting two of my grown children and their families, do the shopping, and take people to their many appointments. We also go to church each Sunday. There is a great deal of driving going on here at the Estate.

All of this running around makes it extremely difficult to keep house. There is a saying that, "A Stay -at- Home Mother ought to Stay at Home!" I agree! Yet there are seasons of difficulties when our best plans and ideals do not measure up to what we would like. So, we make the best of the way things have to be. This will pass. All things do.

As I am driving along, I enjoy the landscape and the prettiness of the day. The weather has been lovely here and I am enjoying being outdoors as much as possible. We have been attending whatever local events are going on as long as they happen while we are already out. I have been walking through little Vermont towns and seeing quaint little shops as our travels require us to be in new places. I am making the best of things and enjoying the hard times.

The home seems to be neglected. I am doing all the basic work I can but have not done much home cooking or baking. My floors need to be washed and vacuumed. This I will get to during the week. It takes a great deal of stamina to do all the work when one is running around all the time. I can only try and make the effort.

My strawberry garden is greatly neglected by me each season. I always try to take care of it, but somehow it manages to survive with little care. Last year, one of my grown sons helped me with the weeding. A few days ago, my oldest daughter worked with me. It is nice to have someone to visit with while doing the work.

This summer looks very busy and I expect to keep running around a great deal. Life is always changing and we have to find ways to remain steady, doing the right and good things despite the trials.

Each week, I will adjust my home routine to do the sweet work of keeping house, while doing my running. Papa will say to me, "Are you running tomorrow?" This is his way of asking if I have to go out and do errands or visits. Papa is disabled and stays home almost all the time. I try to keep my running short and to only certain portions of the day. Then I can be here with him the rest of the time. He is often in the garage, our out on the grounds. I will walk with him or sit on the bench by the strawberry garden. I make an effort to not "do my own thing" so I can sit with him. The family and home need a Mother to be there. The little walks with Papa and sitting by him while he does his projects are a peaceful rest for me. It is a part of keeping house, just being here.

Someday soon, possibly this winter, Papa will ask me, "Are you running tomorrow?" and I hope to say, "No, I will be right here with you, keeping house." Our children and grandchildren will be in and out visiting us. Then I will make a nice old-fashioned pot of beef stew, with fresh buttermilk biscuits and we will sit by the fire and enjoy being home.

17

Exhaustion

I have been struggling with severe exhaustion for quite some time. I know I do far more than I am capable of. It is harder to do all the work of caring for this large house with an almost empty nest. Some days I struggle with the thought that I must be lazy, or why else would I need to rest so much? But then I get some energy back and I am able to do a great deal. Sometimes it is housework, organizing, or baking that I am able to do. At other times, I am able to take care of grandbabies, which is a joy.

Of course, no matter how tired I am, if the grandchildren surprise me with a visit, I will get up and take care of them. I put on a happy face, and slowly make my way to the parlour. They love to help me with my work. The other day, I had to climb on a kitchen stool to reach a pan from the top cabinet shelf. Little 3 -year old grand-girl held onto me, saying, "I've got you Me`me. I won't let you fall." I get more help when the children and grandbabies are here, than when it is just Papa and I to do our work alone.

I have had to give up many things or reduce the time I spend on them – such as writing, making a lot of homemade meals, and little domestic projects. Conserving energy has become a necessity to prevent too many bouts with extreme exhaustion.

Today I was so worn out that I thought, "Well if I must lay down and rest, I will turn on a Charles Stanley sermon and listen while I am doing nothing." It helped refresh me physically and spiritually. Taking things slowly and peacefully is a gift that comes from the struggle for energy. It is a blessing that I get too tired to do much.

18

Domestic Projects

I have been keeping busy with hand-sewing and crocheting. One of my girls asked if I would make her daughter an apron for Thanksgiving. I was delighted to be asked! I went into my dressing room (a little room off my bedroom) and found some pink fabric with little white hearts all over it. I spent the morning setting up the pattern and cutting out pieces, while some of the grandchildren gathered around and watched. I had enough fabric to make a matching mother's apron for my daughter. I use a "ruffles and curves" pattern from "Amelia's Aprons" which I bought more than 10 years ago. It is lovely. The main pattern envelope includes three sizes: adult, child, and doll. It is a simple, easy pattern to use.

Just as I was about to finish the child - size apron, another of my grown girls called and asked if I would crochet afghans for her two little sons. They are ages 1 and 3. I am a little out of practice, so I did a little research and then got to work on a simple, plain pattern. I spent the last week making tiny, baby size blankets in solid colors for my grandsons. One is navy. The other is evergreen. They came out so cute.

As I have been crocheting on the parlour couch, my little granddaughter (3) will sit next to me and hold the yarn. She will ration it out to me, "helping" me as I work. She would help me every time she came to visit (a few times a day). Soon the other children decided they would like me to make them little blankets too. A pink one for grand-girl is what we decided. We will also make purple for another grand-girl, and other assorted colors for the rest of the grandbabies. I will work on these over the next couple of weeks.

I would love to knit a simple set of mittens for each of the children, but I am having a hard time finding a very plain, basic pattern. I wanted something without a cuff that only uses the stitches of "knit and pearl." I will have to keep searching.

On the eve of Thanksgiving, I was just about finished with the Mother's matching apron. Hand-sewing is very time consuming, but a wonderful way to sit and work while still enjoying a visit with the family. Early Thanksgiving morning, after I got our turkey in the oven, I sat down to finish the last of the stitches on the hems of the apron. I was able to give both aprons to my daughter and granddaughter to wear for their Thanksgiving preparations. They looked adorable!

I have to say, I was so shocked and pleased that my girls wanted some "homemade" things. For years it seemed like they only wanted "fashionable store-bought items" for their home and clothing. I was also asked to make a large afghan "for the couch" at my daughter's home. I will work on that soon.

I am seeing other projects I need to work on. My youngest grandbaby is 3 months old. She wears those little store-bought hats which do not look very warm. I will make her a little crocheted bonnet to keep her cozy this winter. She will also get a nice homemade blanket which will be perfect to tuck her into her car-seat.

Homemade projects are a lovely way to pass the time while blessing someone else with a gift.

19

The Children's Bookcase

In the little back parlour I have large bookcases full of literature from the likes of Dickens, Grace Livingston Hill, Margaret Jensen, Laura Ingalls Wilder, stories from the Good Old Days, the writings of Spurgeon, and so much more. Beside one of these bookcases is a box full of children's books. I call it "the children's bookcase." It is full of Amelia Bedelia, The Berenstain Bears, Prayers for children, and many beautifully illustrated picture books. The grandbabies can go into the little room, at any time, and select books to enjoy.

Early one morning, I was sitting in the back parlour reading a Christmas book of memories written by Corrie ten Boom. Soon I heard the sound of little grandchildren coming up the stairs. I placed the book on my chair and forgot all about it as I went to visit with the family.

Later that afternoon, I remembered the book. It was not where I left it. I searched the room and all the rest of the house. It was not to be found. Then I remembered that little 3-year old grand-girl had been in the back room for part of the morning. I went over to the children's bookcase and found that she had taken my Christmas book and had put it away, very neatly, in her bookcase. Such a neat and precious little housekeeper! I couldn't help but smile.

20

Taking Care of Papa

I filled out an application for a handicap designation with the department of motor vehicles. This is for Papa who was in an accident in 2015. His doctor had to fill out the medical portion of the paperwork. It took me several weeks to convince my husband that he needed to be able to park in handicap spaces at the store and pharmacy or wherever else he needed to go. He does not like to think something is wrong with him. He does not want to accept it. But his walking is not always stable, depending on how much pain he is in. A few months ago, he was walking upstairs and, for some reason, he couldn't get one of his legs to cooperate. This caused him to fall on his face. These instances are rare, but they do happen suddenly. He made a wonderful joke about it and we are grateful for his sense of humor. I had been worried he would fall on the ice in the parking lot or slip in some snow while walking into a store. It is hard enough for him to walk inside a store, let alone trying to get in the building from his car. He finally agreed it would be safer to get that handicap parking slip.

I was surprised how quickly the application was approved. He received a permanent parking slip with no expiration date from our state. I was relieved!

Late yesterday afternoon, he asked if I would take a quick ride with him to the local hardware store. He needed a few supplies for some minor home repairs. Even though I had been worn out already from a busy day, I happily agreed to go with him. Someday I will learn that if I don't remember to rest and take it slow, I will have trouble taking care of Papa! I am not much good to anyone when I wear myself out by overdoing things. This outing did not go well.

The first store did not have all that he needed. Papa chose a place closest to our house so he could quickly get back home. I could see that he was already unstable in his walking and was struggling. The second store was a much larger place, but not too much further down the road. We were able to slowly, but surely, get the rest of the things he needed into a shopping carriage. But I was struggling to help. I could not lift anything. I was having trouble finding the energy I needed to get the work done. I started to think that two people with health difficulties are not able to handle errands without an able-bodied person to help them. Next time, we will have to bring one of our grown sons.

Papa started to get irritable as his walking got worse. He was suffering very much. On the way out of the store, the frigid air from outside was so intense that it almost struck me dumb! It made me suddenly useless! It is kind of funny to think about it now, but it was so bitterly cold, I could barely move. Poor papa, who could hardly manage himself, had to worry about me and the shopping carriage and make sure we got to the car safely. He looked at me and said wearily, "I just want to go home and have coffee."

We had all this trouble just for a simple errand. I told him I was so happy we had that handicap parking slip. It would be a big help for these difficult moments.

21

Keeping a Decent Home

These days we are all so busy, we don't have as much time for cleaning our homes. I have read that a housewife in the 40's and 50's used to spend about 6 hours a day in housework. This would include the laundry, the sweeping, dusting, making the meals, and cleaning up the kitchen. Is it possible that we also work that many hours in a day? Hours which are dedicated just to doing the work of home? I might just keep a journal of my hours and work to see how much time it takes me.

A good way to keep the home looking decent, no matter how busy we are, is to keep a list, or a set of basic chore cards in a handy location. There should be work for each day of the week. There could be a laundry day, a dusting and vacuuming day, and a day for baking. I find that working in the early morning is easiest for me, since the family is rarely awake at that time of day. I can easily sweep and wash the floors. Noisy work like vacuuming or doing laundry can wait for the afternoon hours.

I worry that this generation has lost the skill of washing dishes. Many homes have an electric dishwasher. People also tend to use paper plates. This makes learning to wash dishes and keep a clean sink a forgotten chore. In my home economics class, when I was a young teenager, we were taught this essential skill. First, we had to wash the sink. The little filter in the drain had to be clean as well. You were to start the work with a clean area. Next, the sink had to be filled with very hot water. We would add the dish liquid early so it would bubble up, getting nice and soapy. Silverware and cups had to go in first. This was because those were the items that touched the mouth and had to be sanitized in the first of the hot water. When those were finished, we would put in plates and bowls. When those were clean and drying, we would do the pots and pans. We also had to regularly wipe down the dish drainer to keep it clean as well. I have seen so many people dread washing dishes and I believe it is because they don't scrape and rinse the dishes first or clean the sink before they get to work. The water is dirty and unpleasant to work with.

To keep things nice, and to keep the work nice, we ought to start with tidying up the area. This works for vacuuming as well. We need to walk around the room first and pick things up. The room has to be cleaned and dusted before we vacuum. The dirty towels on the bathroom floor should be picked up so the sweeping can be done. The sink in the bathroom should be wiped down and kept nice on a daily basis.

Keeping a neat and decent home could simply mean that we put out fresh towels each day. It means that we don't leave dishes in the sink when we run out to do errands. We try to make our bed each morning before anything else. All these many little tasks of neatness help keep a decent house. This is what makes things pleasant in a home. We have to care enough to do the little jobs of home no matter what trials are going on. This takes perseverance and courage. We should do them cheerfully and with joy. When things are decent, it brings comfort and peace.

22

Old Fashioned Duty of a Homemaker

I was listening to an old sermon on my kitchen radio the other day. The minister was preaching about the duty of a Christian. He talked about what makes a good Christian. At first, we are inspired and excited about our Christian life. . . perhaps we go to Bible study and hear a good sermon. We go out and start living for the Lord based on inspiration. Well, then this feeling (or mood) starts to fade away. If we base our actions only on our feelings, it will not last.

If we still go to church, read the Bible, and pray, even when we are not inspired . . . even when we don't feel like it. . . we are doing our duty. We are building character. We are doing what is right no matter our mood. This is what makes a good Christian.

Do you know what makes a good Homemaker? The same principle of doing our duty as a Christian applies here.

What makes a good Homemaker?

It is when she does the dishes, makes the meals, does the laundry, makes the beds, tends to the children, and cares for her husband, no matter her mood. She does not give - in to laziness, or self-seeking ways of wasting time. She does her work regardless of whether or not she is inspired. If she does her daily work, she is a good homemaker.

She can be an amazing homemaker by going a bit further. She can do this all cheerfully, enjoying the work because she does it as unto the Lord. She may sing hymns, pray as she goes, and make the home look inviting and pleasant because she wants a happy place for her family to live.

My grandmother, from what I am told by my father, was an incredible homemaker who kept a clean house and always did her work. Whenever she visited our home, or we visited hers, she was always tidy and kept her things lovely. Her gracious presence was admirable. She was a preacher's wife (in the 1930's) and the mother of 7 children.   She did not have the distractions we have these days - such as television, computers, or cell phones. She kept to her business of home-keeping. She was a loving wife and mother and a good Christian. She did her duty, and that is what made her great.

Now of course duty can get depressing if we have not love. To keep peace and joy in your life, seek the beautiful life of a close fellowship with the Lord. This will help us stay calm and steady no matter what storms or trials are raging in our life. We can do our work regardless of the mood of the world around us. This is incredibly important!

I have found that singing old time hymns make me happy. Reading the Bible makes me happy. Going to church makes me happy. Doing my Christian duty brings happiness.   When we do our duties of housewifery, we will find contentment and happiness as well.

Being a good Christian and a good homemaker will bring you that peace and joy. They work beautifully together. This old-fashioned duty is what makes amazing, godly homes.

23

The Humble Home

There are many homes with great riches. They have fine furnishings, the best in appliances and fixtures, the plushest carpets, and the brightest and best in glittering lights. The residents in that house have every luxury in food. Their clothing is rich and fashionable. Their yards are perfectly landscaped. Their cars are the new and latest models.

In the off streets, country roads, and out- of- the way apartment complexes, there are many poorer homes. The furniture may be 30 years old but is covered with a pretty quilt or a handmade afghan. The food is basic but nourishing and is often served on an inherited set of dishes, from grandmother's day. The lights may be the dimmer version of a low wattage to keep down the electric bills. There may be laundry on clotheslines on the porch that tend to "blight" the view of an orderly home. The clothing may be an older style, kept decent and neat by mending. The floors and fixtures may be older and plain, but clean. The yards may be humbly landscaped by common labor, rather than by hired designers. The cars are often very old, taking great effort and maintenance to keep them running.

In each instance, whether it be a rich home or a poor one, there still requires a great deal of effort to make it into a "home." This takes mothers and fathers of virtue, kindness, and patience. It takes children who are taught to *work* and to *appreciate* on a daily basis. It is sad to say, but more often than not, the humble home is the school of godliness, where lessons are only learned when we yield to them.

When parents are devoted to the joy of the Lord, whose faces are set towards Him, who giveth all things, it is often the poorer style homes that create strong moral characters and un -worldliness.

These families, from the homes of humble means, are rarely distracted by the glitter of the "best things in life." There are most certainly wealthy homes of benevolence and good works, but those are quite rare in these modern days. It is much more common for a humble home to be a little Heaven on earth, simply because of the family who live there, rather than because of what they possess.

We do daily chores and we ought to have daily religious duties. The family ought to pray at each meal, throughout the day, and before retiring for the night. There should be family altar consisting of Bible reading, the singing of Hymns, and prayers. This is like having a little church in a humble home. The influence of godly actions and living is what will form integrity and virtue in the family. But it must be consistently done.

The holy lessons must be fed to the family every single day because this is what will nourish their souls towards Heaven. Just like we must cook and clean each day, we must do our religious duties each day. If these are forgotten, the family's physical and spiritual health is neglected and in danger.

"It is not with us, as with other labourers," says Puritan minister, John Flavel, "they find their work as they leave it, so do we not. . . Sin and Satan unravel almost all we do, the impressions we make on our people's souls in one sermon, vanish before the next."

Those of humble means tend to rely much more on their Heavenly Father for their daily bread. They have the forced opportunity of drawing closer to the Lord to supply the wants and needs of the home and family.

There is a tremendous load of work – both physical and spiritual, to keep a Humble Home a happy, godly place. Yet, the light of love and warmth will shine brightly in this cold, materialistic world. This kind of home, the one of poorer means, can bring cheer and peace to the family, and to those who enter its hearth.

24

An Evening Drive

One of my girls called in the early evening. She was running low on milk and juice for the children. One day ago, her van had been pronounced unsafe and un-drivable by our local repair shop. She had piled all four of her children's car-seats into my van so I could drive them all home safely. I had gotten used to her coming by to visit a few days a week and enjoyed those visits so very much. Her family had just moved into a home of their own last month. They had just moved out of our large home. I missed them terribly.

We had to make plans to help her get to the grocery store and arrange for me to babysit for when she had errands. But tonight, I knew I needed to buy her some groceries to be sure she and the children had plenty while she was settled at home.

Papa offered to take me out. It was a mild and peaceful drive to the supermarket. We got juice, milk, bread, pizza, and many other things to make them comfortable and happy. These were things we normally bought for them while they were living here with us. It was just part of feeding our family and we were happy to be able to get them what they needed.

It was already bedtime for the children when we arrived at their house. We walked past one of the bedrooms and saw two precious grandchildren surprised and delighted to see us. We tucked them back into their beds, giving them hugs and kisses. We said prayers with them and told them we loved them. It was such a joy to see their angel faces, their happy smiles, and to hear their precious bedtime prayers. Oh, what an incredible joy to be privileged enough to tuck little children into their beds at night and tell them how much they are loved!

Soon we were on our way back home. I want to always remember this very special night, when Papa and I got to help get the grandbabies to bed. This mission work of helping those who need us is the greatest thing we could ever do. All our spare time, all our hobbies, consist of helping to take care of our grown children and our blessed grandchildren. It is a joyful work for which we are grateful.

Notes:

Unit One Project:

Complete a Cleaning Challenge

{Photograph on previous page: The Parlour in Mrs. White's Home.}

Directions for the Cleaning Challenge:

Many of us are in the habit of doing our daily work. The hard part is to get the weekly, heavy cleaning accomplished on a regular basis. Every now and then, it is fun to add a challenge to our routine. This helps boosts morale and provides motivation. Our assignment is to complete a cleaning challenge. I have listed 20 chores. The goal is to finish as many of them as possible in two hours. All you have to do is set a timer for 60 minutes. After the first hour, take a 15-minute tea break. Then reset the timer for another 60 minutes. Start doing the work, as listed below. After you finish each one, put a check mark beside the job. Here is the list:

1 _____ Change the sheets on your bed.

2 _____ Dust your bedroom furniture.

3 _____ Vacuum your bedroom floor.

4 _____ Clean the mirror in your bedroom.

5 _____ Wipe down all the appliances in the kitchen. (Microwave, toaster, etc.)

6 _____ Wash and scrub the stove top.

7 _____ Remove any old leftovers from the refrigerator.

8 _____ Scrub out the inside of the refrigerator.

9 _____ Wash and clean the kitchen sink and dish-drainer.

10 _____ Sweep the kitchen floor.

11 _____ Wash the kitchen floor.

12 _____ Dust the living room furniture.

13 _____ Vacuum the living room floor.

14 _____ Scrub the bathroom sink.

15 _____ Wash the bathroom mirror.

16 _____ Scrub the bathtub.

17 _____ Clean the toilet.

18 _____ Sweep the bathroom floor.

19 _____ Wash the bathroom floor.

20 _____ Sweep or vacuum the front door entryway.

How many items were you able to complete within the 2 hours?

Unit One Questions:

1. Does your home always have to be perfectly neat? Why or why not?

2. Learning to do the dishes is important to keep the kitchen sanitary and healthy. What other things can you do to keep the kitchen sanitary?

3. Taking a meal to a new mother is one way to help someone in need. What else can we make and give to others?

4. Is it possible to set up a routine for homemaking that would prevent you from becoming exhausted or ill? One possibility is to take breaks and stop at a certain time of day. Any other ideas?

Homemaker's Diary

Use this space to write about your experience with homemaking this month. Be sure to share some happy memories of your family.

Notes:

Unit Two

New England Thrift

{Photograph on the previous page: A Covered Bridge in rural Vermont.
The picture was taken by Mrs. White's daughter.}

25

A Rural New England Wedding

Late last fall, a bride and groom began to plan a wedding. The ceremony was scheduled for New Year's Day, on a Sunday afternoon, at the local country church. The pastor spent 5 weeks counseling the couple. Each Friday afternoon, the bride and groom sat down with the minister and were encouraged and advised about a godly marriage.

The bride bought two beautiful large print Bibles from "Sword of the Lord" publishers. She had each engraved with their own names. She had seen her Mother and Father reading the Bible together each evening and wanted that for her own marriage.

The groom worked overtime to earn the money to pay for all the wedding expenses. He provided his bride with money for her dress, the cost of the ceremony, his own new suit, rings, and the marriage license fee.

Wedding invitations were sent out to a small select group of family members. It was to be a very small ceremony. Only 15 guests were in attendance, dressed in beautiful formal attire.

It was a snowy day, so picturesque for a New England wedding. In the sanctuary, the bride's family sat on the left side, while the groom's family sat on the right. Each filled only one pew. The rest of the church was entirely empty. This was an exclusive, private event.

I walked down the aisle holding a tiny grandbaby. I went near the altar to light a white candle, and then went to my seat. There were three other small children in our pew, along with my two grown sons, who looked amazing in their formal suits.

Soon my husband walked down the aisle with our daughter. They both looked so happy. After he handed her over to the groom, he sat down beside me to watch the rest of the service. The minister led us in a traditional wedding ceremony and then introduced the couple to us, as husband and wife.

A photographer took many pictures. The church had lovely Christmas decorations all over the sanctuary, making it look so pretty. In less than an hour, the service was over and we rushed back to our cars to get the babies home, to enjoy a homemade white wedding cake, and to get ready for bed.

The beautiful service and the wedding clothes cost very little. There was no reception. It was just a small and simple ceremony. It was lovely and precious, in a little rural country church in New England.

26

Gifts for Remembering

Papa and I have just returned from a trip to our home state of Massachusetts. We did many things in a short amount of time. There were relatives to visit, sights to see, a wedding to attend, and a campsite to get ready for our rest. We left on a Thursday morning and returned very late in the evening on a Friday night. We had planned to stay until Saturday but got rained out (our tent was leaking). We thought it would be better to stay awake, in the late hours of the night, to get home to our own bed, here in Vermont!

My sister was one of the relatives we visited. She was an incredibly kind hostess. She made sure we were comfortable from our long journey. She had plenty of food for us. She had such a peaceful, kind aura around her that made us smile and rest. The large deck and beautiful fenced - in yard were so nice. We sat at a patio table by the back property and visited. My 80 -year old Aunt was there and we had such a nice visit. My sister bought me a camping survival kit she created, which included bug spray, a first aid box, glow sticks, and m-and-m candy.

We went to see the boats and yachts late in the afternoon that first day. I took many pictures. There is a yacht club in Papa's hometown, so we parked there and stood by the water enjoying the beautiful scenery of endless water and many boats.

Our campsite, in a state park, was heavily wooded. It was peaceful and quiet. We had a nice battery-operated lantern that somehow made the tent feel like home.

The next morning, we went to the cemeteries. We visited the grave of my grandparents, and of Papa's mother. We took time to pray and remember.

Then we went back to the beach town. Papa thought we should go on the carousel and get pictures to show the grandbabies. He thought it would make them laugh. It was such a pleasant ride. The view outside the carousel, through open doorways, was of the ocean. It was so pretty. The music was a gentle, pleasant sound. Every so often, Papa and I, who were each on a different horse, would look over at each other and laugh. The tickets cost $3 per person. It was inexpensive entertainment which we will always remember.

It was pouring rain all that day. We walked down the sidewalk, passing many little shops, an arcade, and a museum. We were both in a great deal of physical pain, especially Papa (who is disabled), but we made jokes and smiled and *lived* despite our suffering. We were on a mission to buy presents to take home to our grandchildren. We had told them before we left that we were going on a trip and would bring back surprises. We didn't want them to be sad while we were away. Soon the beach gift shop was in view. I was so surprised at how affordable and low cost everything was! What a blessing!

We soon found little plastic boats, sand toys, a ship in a bottle, sea shells in a decorative box, and many magnets and postcards. Papa also got me a beautiful little bell with a beach scene and name of the town on the side. Before we had left home, one of our sons (who has a good job) handed me a generous amount of money and said, "Mom, you have fun!" What a treasure!

We had to hustle to get ready for our niece's church wedding. Papa put on his suit and I put on one of my best dresses. It was a beautiful ceremony. Bible passages were read and the couple was soon presented as husband and wife. We were very happy for them.

Due to Papa's failing condition, we were not able to attend the reception. It was time to get home. The drive was very difficult as we were both tired. I prayed for Papa's strength most of the ride home. I know he suffered very much and I was so thankful for him.

We arrived home before 11 in the evening. It has taken us a few days of rest and clumsiness, trying to get our bearings and be back to normal again. We only unloaded part of the car. I hope we can do the rest today.

But despite the pain and suffering of the entire trip, we laughed and smiled and had good memories. We joke through our pain and we pray and thank the Lord for all the blessings we have.

We have souvenirs to help us remember the good. These little gifts of a photo album full of pictures, refrigerator magnets, sea shells, and postcards are precious things which we can look at and always remember the blessing of our trip. These are our gifts for remembering.

27

Doing Less

There is a gentle snow falling here in rural Vermont. It looks so peaceful and pretty as I look out the window. Even though the calendar claims the season as *spring*, it is still winter here in the mountains of New England.

This is a good time to rest. It is a good time to make resolutions for the coming year. Perhaps planning out little gardens to plant when the last of the frost is gone? Maybe think about all the things we would like to do this summer? It can be a happy time of bundling up and sitting near a cozy fire dreaming of spring flowers and sunshine.

I am doing less these days. I remember when all my children were young. They helped me so much with the chores and housekeeping. They did much of the cooking with me and the planning to keep budgets under control. While they learned valuable life skills and work ethics, I had happy comrades to help me in my work.

Now that the helpers are all grown up, I am not able to do all the chores and duties. So, I've had to make changes - find ways of doing less of other things so I could rest more. Of course, there is less work in a smaller household, but there can still be an urgency (in this culture) to multitask and be so busy with projects, making money, and running around that we can become stressed and burdened. Sometimes, we do not even notice this is happening to us until we are forced to stop. Perhaps by a snowstorm or a car that will not work. Sometimes it is by a sickness that forces us to rest. Once we accept these detours (of sorts), and yield to them, we find a benefit of peace and a rest for our minds.

Doing less is definitely the opposite of the race this culture is running. But it gives us time to read the Bible more and to pray more without rushing. It gives us an aura of gentleness and spreads a light of cheerfulness to those around us.

Doing less can mean many things. To me it means I do not want to be swept up with the distractions and glitter of this life that tend to lure me away from a quiet, simple life of a happy, godly home.

28

A Ten Dollar Birthday

I have been getting my parlour ready for a little birthday celebration with my children and grandchildren. I have always shared my birthday with Thanksgiving since it happens in the same week. It is a beautiful time of year when family is expected to visit in just a few days. Often, I seem to neglect to do much for my birthday since the focus is on Thanksgiving.

Very often, we mothers tend to feel disappointed with our birthdays. This sometimes happens if we are overwhelmed or feeling unappreciated. Perhaps we don't think our family will remember the day. This is why it is so important to do a few extra things ourselves to make the day special for others.

I want to see the delight in the faces of my children and grandchildren when I serve a special cake for them to enjoy. I want to have special activities or games so they can have a fun celebration. If we mothers make holidays and birthdays a time of serving our family and a way to bring them joy, we will be so much happier.

We need mothers to bring peacefulness and sunshine to brighten the homes no matter what is going on out in the world. Birthdays are a wonderful time to do just that, even if there is little money available.

Today, I spent just a few dollars to bring some pink cheer to our day.

I spent four dollars at the discount store. I got a pink, plastic tablecloth. I selected cheerful birthday plates and napkins. I also bought a small bag of party favors for the grandchildren to enjoy. It is full of those cute noisy things people blow during New Year's Eve. At the supermarket today, one of my sons bought me a pretty bunch of pink roses from the clearance rack for $3.00. They look simple and beautiful in an old mason jar on my table.

Late this afternoon, some of the grandchildren gave me a lovely homemade present. They had been working with their mother for several days on a hand-sewing project. Their mother had some pretty fabric and sewed a little decorative pillow. She had the children stuff it with cotton. They had a wonderful time helping her. They were so happy and proud when they gave it to me. I was delighted!

Tomorrow morning I will bake a white cake from a box mix. I will also use some chocolate frosting and colorful sprinkles over the top to make it cheerful and festive.

I spent less than 10 dollars for the decorations and the cake. This will bring us all wonderful happiness as we celebrate mother's old - time, simple birthday at home.

29

The Restaurant at Home

I have a set of pretty dishes that came from a Museum. * I have been saving them for just the right time to use here at our Estate. They are so pretty and elegant. I made room for them in the cabinet yesterday. We just started using them. I have to tell you that our home is very humble. It is an old 1850's house that is in need of repairs and general maintenance. I like to bring pretty things here, *humble - old fashioned items*, that bring class and elegance for very little cost. This brightens up our shabby surroundings.

* My dishes came from a community yard sale hosted by our town's museum a few years ago. The entire box cost me $3.00. *

Setting these up in my kitchen inspired me to get back to the old-time tasks of making good food for the family.

This morning, I grated mozzarella cheese and made a batch of whole wheat pizza dough, seasoned with oregano, garlic powder, and olive oil. While I worked, there were grown children and grandchildren all around. We talked a little, but when it came time to knead the dough, I sent them into the parlour. I do my serious work when everyone is safely out of the way. The little ones pulled up miniature rocking chairs and put them on the carpet nearby so they could watch.

I set up a fresh tablecloth on the dining table. I put cloth napkins by each place. The children noticed this was not the time for play-dough or games. We were to have a lovely luncheon. Soon the first batch of two pizzas were ready and the children enjoyed a nice lunch.

I was ready to take a break when one of my sons called to say he was on his way over to pick something up. "*Have you had your lunch?*" I asked him. He had not. I told him I would make him a pizza. He was delighted. This son is a chef in a beautiful Vermont Inn and restaurant. He greatly appreciates food made from scratch, with care and love.

By the time he arrived, I was ready to put his pizza in the oven. It was covered with fresh organic spinach and cheese. I started to clean up the mess so my kitchen and parlour were kept neat. This makes me happy. I love to see things looking pretty. I delight in the work.

In the background, one could hear a gentle sound of an orchestra playing hymns from my kitchen radio.

Someone called for me to go out on an errand. I was a passenger in the car and enjoyed talking about what I wanted to bake when I got home.

Once I was back in my kitchen I prepared a white cake with chocolate frosting. Then I put fresh sliced strawberries on a plate, along with a couple of small scoops of mint chocolate chip ice cream. To this was added a delicate slice of the cake. A piece was served on one of my pretty new plates.

After all was clean and neat, I noticed the bananas and thought it would be nice to make banana pancakes in the morning. I looked in the refrigerator and thought of what I would make for the next day's lunch.

In this area where we live, there are very few restaurants. I have been to the Inn where my son works and it is upscale and beautiful. Yet, there is nothing to compare to the humble, old fashioned home where I can bake and cook in my very own restaurant at home.

30

Spring Work at the Estate

We have been walking the property seeing all the work that needs to be done. Some of us did part of the raking. The grounds had been so neglected last season that we still have our 2 acres covered in leaves from last fall. It is heavy work getting it cleaned up. I worked for about 15 minutes before I had to stop. I simply do not have the muscle for it! But I will keep trying on each sunny day!

Some of our grown children have been working to help with the yard work. We also have plans to plant more wildflowers since they take little effort and not much care.

I hope to get out to the back grounds and clean up my little strawberry garden sometime this afternoon. I will wear my gardening gloves and take the rake with me to gently remove old leaves and such.

The grass here is not quite green. It is only starting to wake up from the winter. We often have frost on the ground into May, but we may have plenty of green at the same time.

My 19 – year old son and I were driving down our country road and saw some little ducks swimming in a flooded bit of land. They looked so peaceful with a beautiful view of the mountains in the background. Sometimes I forget how pretty the land is here and how grateful we are to live here.

Mister and I walked a bit around the house and noticed many repairs that must happen this summer. We have neglected them for so long, it has almost become a crisis.   There is some rotting wood around lower window frames. Peeling paint has been ignored more than 10 years which must be addressed. There is very little money to pay for such things and since Mister is disabled, and I know nothing about such things, we will have to find some way to get this work done.

This large old house is very shabby and neglected these past couple of years. But it is a dearly loved, humble dwelling place that I love.

I have not heard any birds chirping outside yet this season. Once I do hear them, I will be so happy, knowing spring is really here!

31

Reducing Household Electricity

I often get up before sunrise. It is so quiet and pleasant at that time of day. We have an LED nightlight in the kitchen which has a sensor so it only comes on when it is dark. This provides a gentle, dim light, which is peaceful. From what I understand, it only uses half a watt of electricity.

It is very tempting for me to sit on the parlour couch, turn on a pretty lamp, and read by the fire while everyone else is asleep. But I have learned this would cost money and is not the time for reading. We can make many different choices for our use of time. Whenever possible, we ought to do that which costs as little as possible. We must not waste money. So, instead of turning on the lamp to read, I might do some light exercises, straighten the rooms, or clean out my purse. I do things that do not require much light.

Once the sun starts to rise, I open the curtains throughout the house and enjoy the brightening of the morning. This is the time to read or do whatever requires a good strong light. We use the natural light which the Lord has provided us with. This costs nothing. It also brings a bit of thankfulness for that which God has created for our use.

I rarely turn on the television. We do not have cable, but we use a DVD player. I reserve viewing time for when I am ill or when I am very worn down. I might watch an old black and white movie or something funny such as "I Love Lucy." This might happen once a week. I have also learned not to use my CD player very often. I might listen to a sermon or some old gospel songs just while cleaning the kitchen. Then I listen to the pleasant sound of quiet. That is when I notice nature's entertainment in the chirping of birds, the rustling of the wind, and the rushing of a river on the edge of our property. This too makes me grateful and thankful for the lovely things God has created.

Papa watches movies and programs on DVD, and the grandchildren might watch something during their visits and that is okay. It is a blessing to have this resource to make their lives pleasant. But I would not leave television on, wasting its use when there are other things we should be doing. Children are far happier playing with blocks, coloring at the table, and running around laughing.

In the evening, we try to use only one lamp in this large, old house. We are using LED bulbs because we have found them to drastically reduce our electric bill. I am in awe of the Amish who, generally speaking, do not use electricity. Their simple way of living is admirable. There is a gentleness in life which comes forth when we are not so distracted by artificial lights, electronics, and noise.

Other ways to reduce electricity in the home might include kneading dough by hand, without the use of an electric bread machine. We can hand-mix our batters instead of using a mixing appliance. We can hang up our laundry to dry on racks or on the backs of chairs by the fire during the winter season. Or the clothes can go on a line outside during the warmer months. This saves the cost of an electric dryer. We can unplug anything that is not in use.

There are times and seasons for all things. We certainly need to spend some money on heat bills or cooling costs when necessary. We also need a little light at night. But how much nicer it would be to cultivate wisdom and prudence, using natural, daylight for most things. We can do quiet work in the dim light for evening, when it is time to wind down the day. These things keep our expenses down while bringing peace to our lives.

32

Preparing for Winter in Springtime

We are getting ready to place an order for wood pellets. We buy them once a year, in bulk, for the upcoming winter. This is when they are least expensive. We save up all year long and consider this a yearly expense. It is very difficult to hand over a large sum of money all at once, but we know it will keep us warm during the bitterly cold winter, and that is essential here in Vermont.

We also have repair projects we must accomplish before winter. One of the front picture -windows has slipped from its upper frame. We will find some Yankee way of making the repair and try to seal up the window in some way. There are also doors that need repairs to prevent cold winter air from coming inside.

Repairs and purchases for winter are very important, but I have noticed there is something else that must be done. Every winter I struggle with the lack of warmth and sunshine. The winters are much longer than they are in our home state of Massachusetts. I have been told that Vermonters tend to have a higher rate of sadness or depression because of the lack of winter sun. This tells me I have to find special ways of recreation to help cheer us all along the way.

So, in addition to buying wood for the stove, I will stock up on recreational items. I am thinking a variety of puzzles would be a good idea, and perhaps a few new board games. These will provide much cheerfulness since they can be played with a few people. I will have to remember to say, as one of the grown children walk by the parlour, "Care for a game of cards?" These parlour activities will add such joy to us during the confinement of our bitter winters!

For quiet recreation, I will have to organize some of my things to make it easier to sew, practice my violin and my small piano. Years ago, I used to draw and paint. Some of these things I have not done in decades. Perhaps I should acquire some supplies and set up an area for such pleasant productivity.

I also love to listen to Christmas music all winter, and also watch Christmas movies. My favorites are older, classic, often black-and-white movies from long ago. They are wholesome and endearing. I hope to slowly build up a collection of such things to help add to the cheerfulness of homemade winter sunshine.

These are my goals this spring to plan for a pleasant winter. I will make lists and work on them over the coming weeks and months. Each year I try to make our winters better. I believe this idea of adding happiness through indoor recreation may just be the answer to heal the winter blues.

33

The Birthday Drawing

One of my grandsons is turning 2. I had been trying to get to the store to buy him a card. He lives too far away for me to visit, or to bring him a gift. The weather has been bitterly cold here with much snow and wind. At these times I consider myself to be a "shut-in" since I cannot go out. But how would I get a card for baby?

Late one night, I decided to draw him a birthday picture. I used a pencil for the main drawing and then colored pencils to keep it interesting and as colorful as possible. It was just a simple drawing, with the usual birthday wishes and an assortment of balloons all over the page. Next, I used another paper to draw a few large, plain, pictures for him to color. I know he will be happy when he sees it. I also included a trifling sum of money for which his mother may use to buy him a little treat.

Perhaps I will make the birthday drawing a new tradition for the grandchildren who live out of the area. I will most certainly enjoy doing the simple artwork.

34

Summer Days with Small Children

We have been enjoying having the children and grandchildren over quite a bit the last few weeks. Summer days are a relaxing time to enjoy the outdoors and the peaceful pace of the season.

It is good to have a routine to prevent grumpiness in the family. Children can get overwhelmed with all the activity and they may get over-tired. A routine and a schedule can help prevent this.

When I was growing up, all the mothers in the neighborhood were home. I had relatives who lived on our street, as well as on a few streets over. We would get together for picnics in our front yard. There was watermelon and just happy times of playing. We children would walk around the neighborhood, going to the corner store and to the private beach at the end of our Massachusetts street.

We were always delighted when the ice cream truck would drive down our road. We would be outside playing and hear the bell. Since we lived on a dead-end road, we knew we had time to run to our Mothers for some change. Then we would run back out to the sidewalk and wait with the money in our hands. We would just stand there, like good, sweet children, waiting patiently. Soon we would hear the bell ringing and the truck would be heading back to us. We loved taking our time choosing which treat we wanted.

When my own children were growing up, times were very

different. There were not so many mothers at home anymore. But I kept a traditional summer routine, much like the one my mother had for us.

We would get up early and have our breakfast before the heat really settled in. Any chores or baking had to be done in the morning hours. I often started the process of supper before we got too tired. This might be peeling potatoes, putting them in a large pan and filling it up with water. I could just put a cover on this and let it sit until three in the afternoon when I started making the evening meal. I was always a slow worker and wanted plenty of time to do the job. When there was a lot of time available, there was less stress. There would always be interruptions. Children would want to hear a story, or someone would need a Band-Aid. Perhaps the phone would ring. (This was before caller ID and before answering machines.) I would make the call brief because the focus at this time of day was family and the dinner hour. Most people understood that the evening time was just for family and the peaceful routine of winding down the day. Slowly and peacefully the kitchen work would be accomplished.

Throughout summer days, the children would have time to play outside. I would often sit nearby while they played and laughed together. They always did something cute or entertaining that brought me a great deal of joy!

Sometimes I would encourage a new game if they were getting bored. I would show them how to set up some toys and get them started. This would quiet them down and they would get back to their play. I tried not to let the children get "too riled up" because it would wear them out so much that they would get grumpy. Children need peace and gentleness. They need mother with patience and wisdom.

The children would need plenty of juice and light snacks. Lunch was always at around noon each day. Then it was time for naps and rest in a nice cool room. Often, the children needed to hear a few stories to help them to relax before their nap.

A nutritious snack and more juice would be served after this. We always had the children fold their little hands and bow their heads in prayer for all meals and snacks. It was so precious to see their little happy faces as they did this.

Soon they were back outside in the fresh air and sunshine. If there was a baby, we would often just settle in the shade on a blanket or with a carriage (stroller). We would usually stay outside for about an hour at a time and then come back in to rest or to play indoors.

I always had the children help me with the chores, whether it was folding towels, sweeping the porch, or doing the dishes. The children enjoyed helping me because we all did it together and talked and smiled. I would praise them for their hard work and they would feel proud of themselves. They needed to feel they were helpful and doing good things.

If it was very hot, there would be plenty of Popsicles served throughout the day. But we only ate at the kitchen table. This helped keep the house neat and clean. Of course, the children were also welcome to have their treat outside and we often did this with watermelon at the picnic table.

The children loved to play with bubbles, little kiddie pools, beach toys, toy trucks, and baby dolls. They could play for long periods of time if only a few items were offered. This way they were not overwhelmed. I would often help them clean up their games after use. This helped in two ways:

1. The work was kept up to keep things generally in order.

2. If everything was put away several times throughout the day, the children were always delighted to start fresh and play. (Usually if the toys are left out and there is a mess, the children don't seem to notice their games and get bored. But if it is all cleaned up they want

to play all over again!)

The main focus of the house was on the happiness and peacefulness of the family. If there was yelling or quarrelling among the children, it didn't last long. All childish troubles were gently calmed with encouragement, wisdom, patience, and a great deal of understanding and love.

After supper, it would be bath time. Soon the children would be cozy in their pajamas. There was quiet play in the living room with perhaps a time of reading. Sweet, sleepy children would be tucked into their beds with a prayer, a hug and kiss, and a gentle encouragement of a "goodnight. I'll see you in the morning."

These days, I am hearing that this kind of childhood is not so common in our culture. Many mothers work outside the home. When children are not in school or daycare, they attend something called, "day camp" in the summer months. I very much appreciate that this is available for the working parents. But I can't help wondering what little ones are missing out on, when they are not able to have carefree summers at home, year-after-childhood-year, with Mama.

35

Planning Humble Meals

My mother used to make the same food each week. We never got tired of her home cooked dinners. She would make spaghetti and meatballs on Wednesday, Chicken and mashed potatoes on Thursday, etc. I don't think my mother ever introduced a new recipe or any "gourmet dish" to the kitchen table. The food was familiar and comforting. It was all we knew, and we were happy.

Years later, when I became a mother, I would make a list of menus on a piece of notebook paper. I would write down what we were having on Monday, Tuesday, Wednesday, and all the other days of the week. This was posted to the refrigerator door. It helped me to plan what I needed to do in the kitchen. It was also helpful to the family to see what they would be eating.

Some might find it helpful to write out individual menus on 3 by 5 index cards. It might look something like this:

On the front of the card would be the full recipe:

Mother's Beef Stroganoff *

1 pound hamburger	1 package egg noodles
1 can beef broth	4 oz sour cream

Fry hamburger until browned. Add beef broth. Bring to a boil, and then simmer for about 10 minutes. Cook noodles according to package directions. Drain and return to pan. Toss with a little bit of vegetable oil, and then add hamburger/ broth mixture. Stir in sour cream until well blended. Serve hot.

On the back of the card it could say the full menu:

Mother's Beef Stroganoff

Tossed Garden Salad
Tea, milk, or coffee

This could be served every Tuesday evening, for example. A card for each of the seven dinners would need to be created. These are done using your family's favorite meals, the ones you grew up having in your childhood home, or just the meals you constantly make. No need to always wonder what is for dinner or what new recipe you might try.

The recipe on the front of each card will be used to help create your week's grocery shopping list. Then, perhaps you could write out a pretty note of the humble meals you will be serving in your kitchen. This could be always posted on the refrigerator. A change in meals would perhaps be reserved for holidays and special occasions.

This is just a simple suggestion to organize the work in mother's kitchen. It is a way to keep the menus familiar and special. Good old-fashioned home cooking may seem ordinary but it is dearly needed in our homes. I very often hear people wish they could have some of grandmother's meatloaf, or mother's chicken soup. These are tried and true dishes that many families crave. We are also in great need of a return to vegetables, salads, and fresh fruits. We need simple oatmeal and wholesome goodness in our kitchens. Humble, homemade meals, made with love, are the trademark of old- time kitchens.

"Mother's Beef Stroganoff" is one of my recipes that I make for my family.

Strict Economy

The poorer one is, the harder one has to work. It takes a great deal of labor and creativity to be careful in our spending.

Yesterday, the grandchildren wanted pizza. Poor families do not have store-bought frozen pizza available for such requests. So, with the encouragement of my daughter (the children's mother), I set to work in the late morning, to make pizza dough. Someone offered to grate the mozzarella cheese. (It is often cheaper by the block.) Grating cheese is backbreaking work, so one of my grown sons did the job. At some point, after working with the dough, and getting everything set up, I started to wear out. I smiled at my daughter and said, dramatically, "I can't go on." So, I took the 5-month old baby from her, while she took over in the kitchen. I rocked the baby in the chair and sang to him, while the other children ran around the parlour and played. Soon, I was okay enough to get back to work in the kitchen. Baby was returned to his mother's arms.

The pizza was wonderful. I made a few extra and put them in the refrigerator for those who were not home at the time. They were so surprised and happy when they found, later on, that Mom had made them special food.

Another way to live on a limited income is by accepting the fact that one cannot go out much. We cannot waste gas by driving unless it is a necessity. We also have to find our happiness in home amusements. In my childhood home, we would spend hours outside on our acre of land that had a glimpse of a view of Boston Harbor. Reading, drawing, and painting were some of the things I enjoyed doing. These used to be called "accomplishments" if one had training in these recreational activities.

In a simple home with little money, it's good to have drawing pencils, paper, books, and perhaps, if possible, an instrument or two to play with. Hymn books with patriotic and Christmas songs are wonderful to sing for fun. Singing with the family boosts morale.

Making homemade cookies and simple desserts make people happy. These can be done with basic ingredients and an old-fashioned cookbook.

It is also good to have board games stored in a cabinet or kept on a shelf. These will last many years. Games like playing cards, traditional Monopoly, Boggle, Yahtzee, and checkers are important to have on hand.

Living on a tight budget doesn't mean there is deprivation and misery. It doesn't mean one is a tightwad or a scrooge. It means that we make adjustments to living under that income, while finding our happiness in living a joyful, old-fashioned home life.

37

Feeding the Family

Home Economics training for young ladies used to be essential, especially when it came to feeding a family. Girls studied nutrition, cooking, baking, and careful shopping. We need to start focusing on this again.

There was a wonderful market in my hometown in Massachusetts. It was called, "The Fruit Center." It was a beautiful store and contained the freshest quality produce you could find. (Across the street you could see the harbor with a little public beach, and, off in the distance, was a view of the city of Boston!) The prices were affordable, and the displays were inviting. Quite a few homes had small gardens in this suburban area, but when we needed to supplement the harvest, or buy things out of season, we went to "The Fruit Center."

Here in rural Vermont I am finding it harder and harder to find delicious fresh food all year round. I can understand why many grow their own food and preserve it for the winter season. However, I did manage to freeze some of the strawberries and blueberries from my tiny gardens this summer.

My Mother did a marvelous job feeding us nourishing food throughout our childhood. We always had milk and orange juice. She cooked wonderful, comforting suppers for us every single night.

Breakfast was always nourishing and our lunches were mostly eaten at work or school. She was very careful with her grocery budget and made sure we had quality food to eat. She would not buy junk food. If we wanted something foolish like that, we had to use our own money.

There is a sort of laid back attitude these days when it comes to providing food for our kitchens. I see a lot of young adults buying mostly processed food, frozen convenience dinners, and lots of pizza. They are buying what is easy and not necessarily what is healthy.

I remember watching an old episode of "Happy Days." After all the family sat down for dinner, the youngest child grimaced when looking at her plate. Mom had made liver. (shudder) It was more common for homemakers to serve nourishment for the evening meal, rather than what everyone wanted. I don't remember my mother asking any of us what we wanted to eat. She just made the food and we ate it. Of course, she would notice when we enjoyed something more than usual - such as her spaghetti and meatballs! But always, there were fresh vegetables along with a good, hot, homemade meal.

I once read of Rose Kennedy ordering her dinners at home by telling her servants what she wanted. In the morning at breakfast time, she would go over her plan for the evening meal with the paid staff. It was up to them to make sure any shopping or cooking was done in plenty of time to serve the food.

In the instance of a wealthy family with a hired cook or a homemaker doing her own work, there is a requirement of planning, budgeting, and overseeing the work of providing good, nutritious food for one's household.

This should not be taken lightly. It will take hours of work each week to shop, write lists, plan meals, and then to actually prepare food each and every day of the week.

To make this work more pleasant, we ought to find ways to enjoy the shopping and the kitchen duties.

I try to shop in my favorite stores when they are not very busy. That way I can take my time. Sometimes I have grandchildren with me. At other times I might have a grown son who will help me with the unloading of groceries. Rarely, though, do I shop alone. I find it more fun to have company when I do necessary errands.

Our kitchen ought to be inviting and pretty. It should be the place we will enjoy spending a great deal of time. My old-time cabinets are painted a light purple. It is a cheery kitchen which makes me smile. I enjoy baking and cooking while sitting on a tall kitchen chair. I have my radio nearby so I can listen to old time gospel singing or sermons on CD. My parlour table is in sight as I work. I try to make it all clean and pretty so I can work in a happy, pleasant environment.

Feeding our guests and family good, quality food does not have to be expensive. It does not have to be fancy. Basic, recurring menus are perfectly okay and used to be common in households.

I am planning to stock up on several items over the next few months for our long, cold winters. I will have to reorganize my shelves and cabinets to make room. I will also make a list of basic "inventory" items so we can avoid running out of things in case I forget. I am just about to make a weekly menu, something I haven't done for quite some time. I have been slacking on being efficient and wise in my kitchen work. Lately, I have not been taking it seriously. I have fallen into the common ways of being too laid back.

I have to say this.... I believe part of the sliding of kitchen values has to do with the lack of a supper table. People are eating on the couch in front of the television more now than ever before. I have even heard of many people who never even use their table. Let's bring back the old-time family meal at mother's table!

This effort is just another adventure in homemaking. It is something we can do with a smile. We can take care of ourselves and our families by doing the necessary work of shopping and baking and cooking.

I am off to bring a revival to my kitchen!

38

A Winter Break

Here in the mountains of rural New England, it is quiet and peaceful. Each day, this past week, there has been a steady amount of snow throughout the days and nights. It is not a blizzard, but a pretty, gentle accumulation of glistening white to brighten the landscape. It is lovely to see.

The boys have been shoveling out the cars and keeping the parking area, and walkways, in good order. They are often doing this just before the sun sets as they wait for dinner to be served in the evenings.

It is better to stay off the roads during these snowy days. Errands and appointments are rare, or cancelled, as we wait for warmer weather.

I have been catching up on some organizing and heavy cleaning. I have also been doing a lot of reading. It is warm and cozy indoors with our wood pellet stove.

Often, in the early afternoon, I welcome grandbabies to the table. I serve lunch or some homemade treat. It is lovely to have company, especially when it is family!

Our pantry and refrigerator are full of the basics for cooking and baking. I have no need to go to the market, for which I am grateful.

The other morning, my daughter wanted to bake a cake. She didn't have a mix, so I got out my cookbook and showed her some easy recipes using what we had on hand. You can make just about anything, on a whim, if you keep a steady supply of basic groceries, such as cocoa, powdered sugar, flour, and shortening. All we have to do, is put on an apron and get to work.

In Pioneer days, settlers did well in the cold season if they stocked up on coal or wood, for their heat, to last through the winter. They also stored the summer's harvest in a cellar, or on pantry shelves, since they knew it would not be easy to get supplies during the coldest months of the year. How nice it would be if we were able to plan our lives around yearly expenses, rather than weekly ones.

This does not mean we can afford luxuries (like hot chocolate, steak, or "name brand cookies"). Just simple basic ingredients so we can make things from scratch. These might include flour and such for muffins, pancakes, and quick breads. We can even make our own pizza if we have cans of plain tomato sauce and some inexpensive hand-grated cheese. Getting good prices on meat, here and there, so we can stock the freezer over time will also help keep us safe and cozy at home during the difficult weeks and months of winter. Even if we could put up enough food to last a few weeks, it would be ideal in these modern days.

This is such a lovely time to stay home, putter around the house, do projects, and enjoy the hearth and family. There is no rush or worry to go anywhere. We put off as many appointments and errands as possible until spring. This is the quiet time of year where we can just rest and take a winter break.

39

Poverty in the 1800's

Betsy Moody was the mother of nine children. She lived in a beautiful house in Northfield, Massachusetts in the early 1800's. She was expecting twins when her 41-year old husband died suddenly leaving the family in dire straits. There was a mortgage on the house, but because of favorable laws in those days, the creditors were not able to take away her home. Instead, they took just about all her possessions, including the firewood needed to heat the home, in order to recover the debt.

Betsy was the mother of the famous preacher, D. L. Moody. The way in which she brought up her children and retained the family homestead, as a widow, is inspiring.

Her brother came to her aid by providing such necessary things as firewood. They were also helped by the local pastor. Her older children worked in nearby farms (as was common in those days) to help feed and support the family. The work they did helped them to learn skills and built a tremendous work ethic, making them hardworking, dependable, and successful.

The children were required to attend church services, as were most all children of the time. Their "mother instructed her children in the true religion of the heart that seeks first God and His righteousness."

The foundation of their home was strong in godly living. They also learned compassion and charity from an early age:

"Mrs. Moody was tender-hearted, and the children learned the privilege of giving from their scanty store. The hungry were never turned away from her door and on one occasion when the provision for the evening meal was very meagre it was put to the vote of the little ones whether they should give of their small supply to a poor beggar who appealed for aid. The children begged that he should be aided and offered to have their own slices cut thinner."

The Sabbath was a wonderful time for the children. The older ones worked away from home all week and returned each Saturday evening to be with the family. On Sunday, the family brought a packed lunch and spent the day at Church hearing 2 sermons and attending the Sunday School before returning home. This precious time created a beloved "habit of attending God's house."

The children would bring home books from the church library for their mother to read to them. She, herself, only owned 3 books, including the Bible, a catechism, and a "book of devotions." She also read to the children each morning and prayed with them.

Betsy made home life attractive and pleasant for the children, despite her poverty. She did this by encouraging the children to open their home to friends. While the children played, "she would sit quietly with her mending," and provide a wholesome and pleasant environment of love and warmth.

I am amazed at how beautiful their large house was, yet knowing how cold New England winters can be, I realize the Moody family did not have an easy life. Yet, somehow, through their hard work, independent Yankee work ethic, and great trust in God, they succeeded! It also amazes me to learn that Betsy lived in that same house until she passed into Heaven, at the age of 90!

Her grandson tells us that his father, D.L. Moody, "could never speak of those early days of want and adversity without the most tender references to that brave mother whose self-sacrifice and devotion had sacredly guarded the home entrusted to her care."

*Quotes are from the book, *"The Life of D.L. Moody by His Son,"* published in 1900.

40

Homemade Activities for Children

When my grandchildren come here to visit me, I am always looking for something to amuse them. They enjoy play-dough, coloring, and playing with puzzles and toys, but sometimes they want something different. So, I take them into my room and we look for projects.

I pulled out some old scrap fabric. One of the pieces was of snoopy. The children were delighted. They might just play with the material, or just fold it up and use it with their blocks or dolls. Another time, I will pull out some old books they haven't seen in a while and I will read to them.

I came up with a few new ideas. We often have cardboard boxes from deliveries. If I break these up, we can make miniature play houses for games at the table. I have some contact paper, which is used to line shelves in the kitchen. I could certainly use some of this for homemade wallpaper in our cardboard houses. The children can color walls with crayons, and they can draw windows and such with colored pencils. This could lead to making our own miniature furniture and even a little village church.

Another thing I would like to do is find a pretty glass jar and lid. I need to start filling this up with assorted buttons. I have several loose buttons in my sewing box. I should also be removing buttons off old clothes which are no longer worth wearing. Soon I would have a jar full of buttons which the children could play with. I will also use the buttons for my sewing projects.

The children thrive when I ask them to help me with household chores. Every time my 3- year old granddaughter sees some washcloths, she picks them up and refolds them. She will also dust the kitchen chairs and make beds. The children love to help me keep house.

Sometimes one of the children will say, "We need a snack. What should we make?" We go into the kitchen and start getting the baking things ready for brownies, cake, muffins, or cookies. I love that the children know it takes a little work to prepare food. It doesn't just come out of a bag from the grocery store. When the time comes for me to use the oven, or stove, the children know they must be safe and go into the other room. Or, if they still want to be nearby, they will get their little rocking chairs and sit by the sink, at a good distance from the grown-up work I am doing near the stove. I give them small bowls and spoons with just a bit of water for them to mix to keep them busy. Helping to make the food is a wonderful homemade activity for children.

The children love to help me put the laundry in the dryer. I take out a little bit of clothes at a time from the washer, and hand to a child, who then loads the dryer. This makes them proud of their accomplishments, to help do grown- up work.

It is good for children to learn to sing and to be sung to. All of my children grew up hearing and singing hymns out of the old hymn books we had at home. Recently, when visiting my oldest daughter, who lives a few hours away from me, I held her little 3 -year old boy and sang "Amazing Grace" to him. He sat quietly and was so dear. I only get to see him a few times a year and was surprised he sat still and let me sing to him. His mother said, "Yes, well, he loves that song." I asked if she sings "Amazing Grace" to him. She nodded and said, "I don't know any lullabies. I only know hymns." How precious! I was delighted.

Children like to be creative. They like to build and be productive. They like to keep busy with projects and activities of their own invention. They need plenty of time and quiet to just be children. We can provide them with a happy home and a yard with fresh, clean air. We need to be here to guide and protect them, providing them with nourishing food, structured times of chores, play, meals, and bedtime. This helps produce sweet and happy children.

41

Making Money Last

I was in the hardware store the other day. They had an entire floor devoted to decorative gardening accessories, patio furniture, and pretty benches. There were swimming pools and barbeque sets. It was so much fun just looking at everything. I saw the sweetest little garden turtle. It was a decorative item for the outdoors. It had the happiest, cutest face painted on. I thought my grandchildren would love it. But the cost was $28. So, I just stared at it for a bit and then moved on.

Over the weekend, I was in the drugstore picking up a prescription for my husband. I love to browse around while I wait. They always have such nice seasonal items. I noticed they had a similar turtle as what I saw last week. This one was a bit smaller, but just as charming. It cost only $5. I was delighted and happily paid for it. I plan to put it in the front garden this coming week. I know the grandbabies will love to see it as we tour the grounds on our regular walks this season.

Buying things on impulse can be such a dangerous thing. Our money can disappear so quickly if we are not careful. But occasionally buying something inexpensive, that makes us smile, can be pleasant.

This winter, I took all my saved coins and gave them to one of my grown daughters. It used to be easy to save for a rainy day by filling up jars full of coins. But now the bank won't accept the rolled money. Instead, they direct people to a machine in their lobby. This machine counts all the change and prints out a slip so you can get dollar bills at one of the teller stalls. But the machine deducts a certain amount as a fee. I just cannot fathom paying this. It is such a waste, even if the charge seems small. So, I have been keeping a change purse with me. Whenever I do any shopping these days, I count out the exact change. It takes a few extra minutes, but I no longer have to worry about what to do with a jar full of money that is difficult to spend. The days of saving change for a rainy day seem to be out of fashion.

Since we homemakers do a great deal of the spending in a household, it is important that we find ways to make the money last. Each week, I have been taking my receipts and recording my spending in a journal book. This is for groceries and gas and also any bills I have paid. I want to remember where the money went. This helps me be more careful. I also enjoy remembering some of our adventures by reading old entries. The day I bought the garden turtle and wrote it in the book will make me smile.

Dressing up to do errands or to go shopping was common in earlier days. My mother always did this. She would put aside her housedress and put on something nicer before going out. Rushing out the door all the time to get things we forgot, or to hurry some errand, can cause us to be wasteful. Often, we will be in such a rush that we buy what is convenient or quick. This will waste money. Finances are a serious matter. We need funds for food, housing, and clothing. These are basic needs. But we should treat that money with a great deal of care and planning. I always dress up a bit before going out because I am more careful in what I do. Dressing up a little is part of being prudent. It is part of being cautious and precise in such an important job as spending the household funds to care for the family.

Impulse buying should be so rare that we are thrilled when we actually spend a bit of money that was not planned. This will make us very grateful for the little treats we have in life.

Making money last just means we don't easily part with it. We are slow and careful with our spending decisions. We keep our bills and expenses low so we can have money in a savings account. This is being a wise steward with what we have been entrusted with. It also brings great peace and happiness to make that money last as long as possible.

42

A Penny Offering

I have always loved going to church. There are traditions and rituals that are so comforting as we go through each service. I love the singing of hymns, the prayers, and the time of offering. It has always made me happy to say a little prayer over any money we place into the basket.

When my children were little, I would give them each a dollar bill to place in the church basket at the beginning of the service. As the ushers came around the pews, my children were always happy to put the money in the basket.

In the past few years, some of my grandchildren have been attending services with me from time to time. I always hand them a dollar bill with solemn instructions on when, and how, to place it in the basket. It is so precious to see their little faces when the usher comes by and they, with a bit of awe and pride, place that dollar in the basket. It is money for the Lord. What a privilege for little ones to give!

My husband and I have been in the habit of writing out a check to pay our tithe and sending it in the mail to our church. He is paid once a month for his disability, so it is easier to pay it right then along with all the bills. This means I must have a few dollars handy to give during each church service. This past week, since money was running low at the end of the month, I was caught unprepared. I didn't have money in my purse! I did not want to have that basket come by without my happily giving something towards the Lord's work. It gives me great joy to pray and to give. I quickly searched through the bottom of my purse and found a single penny. This is what I placed in the basket that day. I was so happy to have something to give.

Later in the week, the disability income arrived and I wrote out a check and mailed it to our church, with a little card and a note saying, "I am thankful for our church!" It is such a blessing to give, even if all we have is a penny.

43

A Louisa May Alcott Winter

Here in rural Vermont, the bitterly cold winters remind me of life in Concord Massachusetts as described by 1800's author, Louisa May Alcott in her beloved book, "*Little Women*."

To cheer myself up during these long winter days, I like to read literature from an earlier era to see how others have lived while often snowed - in or kept indoors because of the cold New England days.

I have often read "*The Long Winter*" and other Laura Ingalls Wilder books. But this winter, I am focusing on the sweet stories of Miss Alcott. Last year I read "*An Old-Fashioned Girl*." I enjoyed hearing how visits were made on Winter afternoons and the guests would sit by the fire in a lovely home.

I just watched the movie "*Little Women*" which showed a beautiful house in Concord. The interior was humble and lovely. There are fireplaces in most of the rooms. Pretty wallpaper makes the home look cozy and sweet. The girls wear pretty coats and shawls. They make an old-fashioned home, especially in winter, look inviting and peaceful.

Our Estate here consists of several rooms. Many of them are large and a bit chilly. Some are too cold to spend much time in, so we close them off and try to avoid them until spring. Our wood pellet stove in the upstairs parlour makes the home so pleasant and warm. We also have other sources of heat, such as electric and kerosene, along with a wood stove on the main floor. I have often thought of this house as a humble, Jane Austen, English estate. This winter I shall think of it as a dignified home similar to Orchard House owned by the Alcott family. One must find a way to cheer along dreary days with happy thoughts!

I very much enjoy reading about how New England families, in the 1800's, passed the time at home during the winter. We have our Bible time each evening. We also enjoy table games, singing, and do a lot of reading.

I have been baking a great deal the last couple of weeks. This helps warm up some of the rooms and provides treats for the family to enjoy.

I will be doing a lot of mending, sewing, and writing during this cold season. Our most difficult months are January and February. These are bitterly cold and can be depressing at times. I will focus on the happy stories of Miss Alcott and enjoy our home as if it were a dear old home in Concord, Massachusetts.

44

Dropping Luxuries

Last month, I decided my cell phone was a luxury. I had gotten used to texting my children and receiving photographs of my grandchildren from them. I enjoyed saying "Good morning" and "Good night," with hearts, to encourage them each day. But strict economy must be put into place when the income is low. This meant that a cell phone bill (regardless of how small it may seem) was considered a luxury in life and must be dropped.

It took me a few days to adjust, but since I have only had a cell phone for about a year now, it was not too difficult to get used to the way it was. I decided that the only time I would put a monthly plan on it, was when I have to travel, which may only be once or twice a year. In this case, I would only have to pay for one or two months rather than for 12. That is an enormous savings.

In the last couple of weeks, as it has been so cold out, I have not been able to grocery shop very often. We are searching the pantry shelves and being creative with what is on hand. I have been trying to make coffee cake, and muffins and such, a few times a week. Buying ready- made food and baked goods are a luxury I cannot afford. So, I keep flour and sugar and such things in the pantry so I can "make" what we eat. This is much more affordable, regardless of how tiring it may be.

This afternoon, I will make homemade beef stew and biscuits. I expect it will wear me out so I am resting up before I do the work. I have learned to make the biscuit dough first and get it all ready on a baking sheet. Then I cover them with plastic wrap and refrigerate them to bake later when the stew is ready. This way I am not doing everything all at once. One of the boys helps me with the beef, and then I rest at the kitchen table when I peel the vegetables. I like to sit on a sofa in the parlour and read while the stew is cooking so I can stir it and keep a good watch.

The cost of bread has gone up lately, making it difficult to afford. I hope to bake some bread on a weekly basis, as I am able. I used to do this when my children were little, because I had many helpers! These days, I can often make the dough in the late afternoon, and then refrigerate it. The next day, I can let it rise and then bake it. That way I am not doing all the work in one day.

Whatever simple, nourishing food we can make ourselves will save a lot of money over time. The hard work, though wearying, will build up our strength and keep us healthy. Truly, there is nothing wrong with labor. I often cringe from it, and would rather rest, enjoying ease, but necessity makes hard work essential. There is a sweet reward and a blessing in living a simple life within one's means. This brings great peace.

Buying new curtains, pretty linens, and new dishes to cheer one up in the spring time is a luxury I would love, but cannot afford. So, I will simply clean and freshen what I have, and be content with our lovely old home and our way of life, where very little money is available. Frugality and thriftiness are important and wise. This makes little gifts and notes we receive from others on birthdays and holidays such a special treat. When we give up luxuries for a time, we are so happy when we are able to have occasional surprises.

45

Retirement Planning for the Poor

In my childhood days, living in New England, there were many called "the working class." These were traditional families where Dad worked while Mother stayed home to care for the family. It was a simpler time. (By today's standards, financially speaking, these would be considered "poor" people.)

Mothers were busy making food from scratch. In those days, convenience food was not common. Most Housewives did not trust pre-made frozen food. They had always made their own food and felt it was wholesome and nourishing. Mother took pride in feeding and caring for her husband and children.

These Mothers deep cleaned their homes on a regular basis. They mended the family clothing. They were productive at home doing things that did not earn them any money. The fathers went to work earning the living.

In those days, debt was something to be avoided. But the goal, here in America, was to own one's own home. In the early 1970's, many houses were available for around $20,000. These were lovely homes that were very simple. Once a family purchased a home, they generally stayed there. This established neighborhoods and communities with people everyone knew and trusted. This also gave them security that they had a home which was either "paid for" or would be paid off in the near future.

Owning a home was a big part of financial planning. It brought stability and security. In some families, particularly in Italian homes, once Mother and Dad were older, they would have a grown child still living with them, perhaps a son with his wife and children. This helped them take care of one another. It also kept expenses low since there were more people to share the work and the cost of living.

The house was kept within the family. Sometimes a bachelor son or maiden daughter was still living in the house when the parents passed on to Heaven. It was called "the family homestead," even if it was a small house in the suburbs of Boston.

The biggest investment a family could make was to own a humble home. Planning for retirement meant working for as long as it was physically possible. It meant making sure there was a gravesite for the final resting place. It meant doing one's best to have a basic life insurance policy to cover the cost of a burial.

Things have not changed that much. There are still "working poor" families whose best investment is owning and maintaining the family homestead.   In Scripture we are told that the poor will always be among us. There is certainly nothing wrong with being either poor or rich. There are just different ways of living and planning for retirement.

I have always loved having a house full of people. It is a blessing to have grown children, and even grandchildren, living in the same home. This is what I have grown up with, and what I have always known. (For those who are not familiar with this kind of life, there is an excellent example of this on the television show, "*The Waltons.*")

Middle and Upper-class families may have all kind of investment strategies. There are excellent books which teach all about retirement planning for those with disposable income. It is certainly important and noble to be a good steward of the money one has. But realistically, the working poor are not going to have investment portfolios or plans of retiring from work early. They are not going to have disposable money. And that is okay!

I have seen many of the working poor live beautiful lives of simplicity and godliness. I have seen them live with a focus on their Eternal Home. The contentment they feel is inspiring. They have worked hard their entire lives and passed on the work ethic to their children and grandchildren. Their values of morality, thrift, and charity are admirable and worth emulating.

Sometimes, the main goal of retiring, for the poor, is simply looking forward to that incredible resurrection morning and hearing:

"Well done, thou good and faithful servant. . . enter thou into the joy of thy Lord." - Matthew. 25:21

46

A Spending Freeze

In the 1800's book, "Stepping Heavenward" by Elizabeth Prentiss, there was a time of financial strain in the home. The husband was working very hard to pay off some debts. This required extra care in domestic spending. Food must not be wasted. Sewing was a constant duty since most of the clothing for the entire family was made at home. You would read about the wife sitting in the living room, in the evening, mending and sewing shirts for her husband. She had to "keep him in shirts" so he could go to work each day. The children would need any rips or tears in their clothing repaired on a regular basis. When money is very tight, it requires extra work.

In the book, "The Shaping of a Christian Family," Elisabeth Elliot talks about her childhood home. They "learned a strict frugality in the smallest things." She explains how her family lived on very little money. Her clothing was never new. She owned only 2 pairs of shoes, one being the pair for Sunday best. They were careful with the use of electricity, water, and toothpaste. All the little things were used with the thought of thrift.

This type of living was very common in previous generations. We were taught not to waste anything. It was wrong to frivolously spend money. We had to be careful.

Sometimes when things start to get out of control – perhaps the electric bill was too high, or too much money was being spent on gas for car trips. Perhaps we keep buying things on impulse, or there is not enough money being saved. This is a good time for a spending freeze.

This simply means we go as many days as possible without spending a single dime. We make do with the food in our kitchens, getting creative with the cookbooks, and being careful about portion control. We do not go to the stores. In these modern days, we have to remember to avoid any online spending. We do not buy anything.

This "freeze" is similar to a fasting from food. This month there was a day of fasting. I spent most of the morning with my grandchildren but did not tell them I was fasting. I was as cheerful as I could be, even though I missed food so very much. Every time I thought about how nice it would be to just have a piece of toast, I thanked the Lord for food and looked forward to when the fast would be over. This took a great deal of determination and discipline. It was very difficult. I was so incredibly grateful for the blessing of eating, when the fast ended!

Much like my fast, we will become more thankful and appreciative for the money we have if we go through a period of time without it. If we put aside our income (other than for basic bills of course), not using it for anything more than basic essentials and simple food, we will develop a strong discipline for managing money successfully.

47

Rich and Humble Living

In 1905, a book of moral and religious stories contained a sketch of a struggling family who were in great need of new clothing, comfortable furniture, and home repairs. * Mother did her best with what money and resources she had, but it was difficult and discouraging. When a good sum of money was obtained, she was able to do several things which greatly boosted the happiness and morale of the family. **The lesson here was that times of hardship should be a temporary matter.** It is a blessing and a gift to have pleasant surroundings, pretty clothing, and treats which make one smile, particularly if these can be done with prudence and frugality. We must not pile up an abundance of money, letting it sit idly in savings, when a portion can bring happiness to those around us.

Providing a bit of comfort and pleasantries for daily living does not have to cost a great deal of money.

Happiness may also be obtained in our activities. These past few weeks I have been playing tennis with my grown sons. There is a beautiful court in a lovely park maintained by the town. The only cost I have incurred is the purchase of a set of rackets and tennis balls, which were a small one-time expense. These should last me many years, perhaps even a lifetime. One often feels rich when one takes even an hour a week to enjoy some outdoor recreation in season.

We can slowly add material items to our homes and lives, over a long period of time. These may be a set of pretty curtains, lovely dishes, cheerful paint for a hallway, elegant pictures for an entryway, games for the parlour, and yes, even a set of tennis rackets.

Amy Dacyczyn, in her book, "The Tightwad Gazette," teaches that we can add things to our lives on a yearly basis that will help save us money, and also make our lives better (such as gardening tools, a set of quality baking pans, a sewing machine, cloth diapers, a good dress-suit, fruit trees for the back yard, etc.). The method is to take a small amount of money in the first year to frugally purchase what is wanted (or needed) and then each year, purchase the next thing on your list, and on and on. Over time, with lots of hard work and patience, you will have the desired items to make your life better (and happier).

Some may think that being poor, or of humble means, suggests that being "lower class" should be taken literally. This is rarely the case. In the history of our American ancestors, many started out in humble cabins yet were people of virtue and good citizenship.

Evangelist Dr. John R. Rice (1895 - 1980) was a very rich man when it came to family and friends. He is quoted as follows:

"You say, 'Crime is excusable because somebody is poor.' I was poor, too. My family was poor. I wore "hand-me-down" clothes. Eight of us lived in a four-room country house without plumbing, without electric lights, without running water; and we were decent and honest, and went to church, and paid our bills, and did right. Being poor doesn't give any excuse to break the laws of the land."

Abraham Lincoln is well known for coming from a childhood of poverty and humble means. He went on to become the President of the United States of America. His son, Robert, became a wealthy businessman who built a beautiful mansion in Vermont.

Poverty is often as temporary and fluctuating as the stock market. Things get better! We can live rich lives through the good times and the bad, depending on our attitude and outlook.

There is something called, "the joy of the Lord," which will greatly help us in our attitude. This is a life of strong faith and trust in Almighty God. He owns the cattle upon a thousand hills! (Psalm 50:10) He feeds the birds! (Matthew 6:26) And just like the old, sweet hymn says, "His eye is on the sparrow, and I know He watches me."

* *"Sabbath Readings for the Home Circle"*

48

The Housekeeper's Budget

As another month draws to an end, it is time to reflect on the household budget. I am ready to close out this month's account. This is where I add up all the bills that were paid, the money I spent, and the money I gave away. Every dollar and dime are accounted for because I write it in a book. This helps me see what I am doing wrong, or how I can fix things for the coming months. It also keeps a record (or a history) of our home expenses.

A good housekeeper must be a good manager. One of the biggest goals she should have is to live on a budget. She must learn to live within the income the house is provided with. This takes time and effort. It even takes a great deal of wisdom and logic to avoid the traps and temptations of the advertising world around us.

We are taught, in our modern world, to save money by spending it. This is a genius advertising method to get us to spend as much money as possible. There are many ways to save money and we must learn to be creative and find what works in our own situation. For instance, I can tell you how to save money on winter heat here in Vermont. But it will not help someone living in Florida. We can share ideas on how to save, but we must take only the advice which works for our own family.

We had a couple of high bills outside of our budget recently. A car repair bill (which I consider to be part of a yearly expense) was more than I expected. There were also a few emergency trips which cost extra money in gas and charity. This put me over my spending. Since we live on a fixed income, I had to take the extra money out of a small savings account to make up the difference. This is not good because that savings cannot be replaced. So next month I have readjusted my expenses to keep my spending low. One of the biggest ways I did this was to cut my gas and grocery money. This means I will have to work much harder in making homemade meals and to stay home as much as possible. These are not difficult things to do, but they do take time and effort. They also require some sacrifice on my part. I am willing to do this because it will help our family and home for the long term.

I could either be wasteful and foolish or I can be frugal and careful. I choose to work here at home, doing my part, to keep us out of the poor house. Every housekeeper ought to have that same attitude. The lady of the house can spend her family into poverty or she can manage the money well and bring peace and security into her home for many years. The stability of a home depends on how well the household funds are managed.

Does it matter if you are poor or rich? In other words, is it okay to be careless and carefree and wasteful in our management of money just because we have plenty? Being frugal and a good manager of one's income is something every single household should practice. No business will last long if they spend more than they make. No household will stay out of the poor house if they spend more than they make. One should not make a habit of spending out of the savings account or of getting into debt to get through the month. All of us have to live within our income.

I want to explain the importance of little savings. We can earn a few pennies in a savings account. We may look at our bank statement and think it is a paltry, insignificant income. However, if you think about that interest earned in a new way - you may be more likely to appreciate every little dime.

1. I have been paying my electric bill over the phone with a check (or debit card) for over a year. There is no fee. There is no cost. This has saved me one stamp per month. That is like earning 48 cents in interest for the month.

2. I just learned that I can also do this with my phone bill. This will save me another stamp and earn me another 48 cents.

In these two items I have earned almost a dollar by doing something different. That is 12 dollars a year which could buy a gift for someone's birthday. It is by being creative and by being careful with money that we can be successful managers. Can we face most all things in our financial life in a similar way? Could we try to spend less in every aspect of our household without really changing our quality of life?

The housekeeper's budget is just a simple notebook listing all the fixed expenses like the rent or mortgage. It includes the electric bill, the phone bill, and the cost of insurance. There is an amount for groceries and gas and any other expense that is required to run one's home.

Another book could be the "house account" book where all the money that is spent is recorded as they happen throughout the month. This is where we see the truth of how the budget is working. We can see any mistakes we make or any changes that are necessary. It takes a bit of thought and time to keep household financial books, but they are an important part of managing a home with care and wisdom.

Unit Two Project:

Set up a House Account

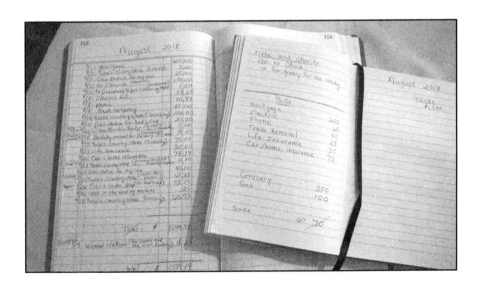

{Photograph on previous page: A fictitious example of Mrs. White's
Account Books.}

Directions for Setting up a House Account:

Keeping a ledger of household accounts was a common practice. Sarah Edwards, wife of Puritan minister Jonathan Edwards, was said to have provided historians with a detailed picture of their spending because she wrote down every single transaction.

"It was a happy circumstance that he could trust everything to the care of Mrs. Edwards with entire safety and with un-doubting confidence. She was a most judicious and faithful mistress of a family, habitually industrious, **a sound economist, managing her household affairs with diligence and discretion.**" - *Marriage to a Difficult Man - The Uncommon Union of Jonathan and Sarah Edwards"* by Elisabeth D. Dodds

Did you ever see the movie, "Little Women" starring Susan Sarandon? You will see them, at times, leaning over a household ledger account.

Edith A. Barnett, in 1894 (London) wrote a book called *"Primer of Domestic Economy."* Here is a quote from this document - "Whether the income be small or large, certain or uncertain, the good housewife will keep an accurate account of her income and expenditure." She also wrote this: "Probably women as housekeepers spend the greater part of the money that is spent in the world."

Assignment:

Set up a House account for one month. You will need two books. One is a "ledger book" or "cash book." This is where you will write down all your spending. The other is just a plain journal or notebook. It is for the monthly budget.

House Account: The Ledger book.

1. Write down every single cent you spend. I prefer to use a "ledger book" or something with 2 columns. At the top of the first page, write the month and the year. Each time you spend money, write down the date, a description, and the amount. Here are some examples from the photograph on page 127:

8/1/2018   Paid the Mortgage $600

8/3/2018   Rose's Country store (snacks) $3.00

8/5/2018   Gave to Grandbaby to put in the offering basket at church $1.00

8/8/2018   Paid the Electric bill $58.25

8/17/2018   Rose's Country Store (groceries) $75.00

8/23/2018   Gas for my car $40.00

8/26/2018   Lost in the Vending Machine   .25 cents

2. Keep receipts of all your purchases. Transfer these to the ledger book at the end of the day, or when you get a chance during the month. I also transfer my debit transactions, and any checks I have written, into the ledger book.

   Sometimes I am able to record everything at the end of the day. At other times, I might do it once or twice a week. This is always a good excuse to clean out my purse and discard the receipts as I write them down.

   I keep a small notebook in my purse where I can write any spending, or loss of money, in case I don't get a receipt. I will also write down if I gave a few dollars to one of my grown children, so I can put it in my ledger book when I have time.

3. I never write down what my husband spends. My purpose is to keep track of what I am, personally, doing with money. However, if I give him cash for gas or whatever, I will put in my ledger book, "gave money to Papa... $10."

4. I include the household bills in my ledger book only because I am the one who pays them out of my husband's income. If he did the bills, I would not include them in my book. Again, I am only recording what I am, personally, doing with the money I am given.

5. At the end of the month, look this over and add up your spending. Put the total at the bottom of the page. I don't do categories of spending, I just write the total of all that has been spent.

6. Sometimes, after I have already written down the total for the month, I find an odd receipt, or an entry in my notebook. I will add this in at the bottom of the page, along with a new total. In some cases, I spend more money than my income allows (as you will see in the photograph on page 127). In this case, I would have taken money from savings to make up the difference. The record helps me see where I can cut back and do better next month.

7. Be willing to share this book with your husband.

House Account: The Budget

The second book is for the budget. This is the plan for the month. You can use an ordinary notebook or a pretty journal. In the photograph on page 127, my budget is written inside a pink, imitation - leather journal, with a ribbon marker.

1. You will need to use two pages for each month. The left side is the budget and includes space for notes. The right side is to list the income and any notes.

2. On the left page, write down all the bills, as well as the amount you intend to spend on groceries, gas, charity, and any savings.

3. On the right side, write down the Month and Year.

4. On the right side, write down the expected income for the month. In my household, we receive our income only once a month. When we used to receive a weekly amount, I would break down what to do each week. I will give you an example based on the photograph of a budget on page 127. The month's income is listed as $1,500, which is $375 each week.

Week one income: $375.
Expenses to pay for this week:
Gas $25
Grocery $87.50
Save for Mortgage $150
Tithe $37.50
Car/ Home Insurance $75
Total: $375

Week two income: $375.
Expenses to pay for this week:
Gas $25
Grocery $87.50
Save for Mortgage $150
Tithe $37.50
Life Insurance $30
Trash Removal $25
Save $20
Total: $375.

Week three income: $375.
Expenses to pay for this week:
Gas $25
Grocery $87.50
Save for Mortgage $150
Tithe $37.50
Electric $60
Save $15
Total: $375

Week four income: $375
Expenses to pay for this week:
Gas $25
Grocery $87.50
Save for Mortgage $150 (Pay the mortgage this week.)
Tithe $37.50
Phone $40
Save $35
Total: $375

This is just a plan to pay all the bills throughout each of the four weeks of income. You can cross them off as you go along. Sometimes the savings amount is crossed off and changed if money is used for grocery, charity, a repair, etc. (You will see an example of this change in the photograph on page 127.)   It is good to make notes throughout the month as the budget will often change.

Each new month, I write a fresh budget so I can follow our plan and keep track of everything I have to pay.

Unit Two Questions:

1. Did you keep a House Account this Month? How did it work?

2. Playing checkers, cards, and other games doesn't cost anything. What type of recreation can your family do that does not cost much?

3. Wearing cozy sweaters and having warm blankets is important for New England Winters. What ways can you reduce your heating costs this coming year?

4. Happiness and peacefulness have a lot to do with having a good outlook, especially when money is limited. What can you do to keep your family cheerful during tough financial times?

Homemaker's Diary

Use this space to write about your experience with homemaking this month. Be sure to share some happy memories of your family.

Unit Three

To Be A Lady

{Photograph on previous page: Tea Table in Mrs. White's Home.}

49

Tea Time:

The Importance of Formal Ceremony at Home

I usually have tea in a regular coffee cup. It is almost always plain "Salada" tea. I do not take cream or milk. I only add a small amount of table sugar. In my healthier days, I would drink peppermint tea with honey (never sugar). Recently, for special occasions, I have been using dainty china cups.

I will not have "tea time" unless some of my grandchildren are present. I do this to entertain them, to teach them manners, and to help them develop a sort of refined culture in daily life.

I will say to Miss Grand-girl (currently age 3), that I would like to have tea. This is usually after we have done some chores together and have colored with crayons. She immediately says, in a rather dignified way, "*okay.*" And immediately walks over to the hutch to get my tea cup and saucer. She places it on the table for me, and we begin the process of preparing a "formal" tea.

I have to say that I was very hesitant to let her handle my fragile dishes. But after a few lessons at the sink washing some of them, she has proven to me that she cares very much and will try very hard to be cautious. I also have to say that I am willing to give up any of my china and dishes with a sympathizing smile should there be an accident. In other words, if Miss Grand-girl drops and breaks my cup or plates, I will gladly take the loss. After all, at the end of life, we cannot take *things* with us.

At the table, there is a sugar bowl. Just for fun, I have this filled with sugar cubes. This is the "company best" sugar that adds to the fun of tea time. I will say to one of the grandchildren, *"I would like one sugar please."* They take turns getting me a cube and placing it into a tea cup. This delights them!

We always use linen napkins. Some are homemade, some are store bought, and others have been given to us. These are neatly folded and kept on the hutch or sideboard table. The children will get one for each of us. *"These go on our laps,"* I tell them. We also have extra napkins on the table beside our plates.

I keep a "creamer" container on the table which is always empty. It is there for *looks*, since none of us take cream or milk in our tea. Perhaps in winter I will fill it with miniature marshmallows and turn "tea time" into "hot chocolate time."

There is a silver call bell at my place setting. This is what one would use to call the maid to the table or ask for help. Since I am the only maid, I ring the bell to make the children smile. I might say, *"Time for tea,"* just before a ring. Or I might say, *"lunch is served"* and then give the bell a little shake. The children find this endearing.

In my kitchen, there is a small canister full of flavored teas. The children and I have enjoyed papaya, and apple cinnamon the most. I give the children only a taste with a teaspoon, and then I drink the rest. They love the scent, the fancy cups, the sugar cubes, and watching the steam. Then they are happy to enjoy juice and a treat in their own seats at the table.

We sit up straight, we talk politely, and we say our prayers with folded hands. We ask each other, *"Is there anything else you need?"* or *"Would you like some more?"* Here at the tea table, we learn to take care of each other. We learn to be kind and considerate.

Tea time is very short, but the lessons extend to meals. The children always use linen napkins at grandmother's table. We always use our very best manners, whether it is breakfast, lunch, or dinner time. This does not mean that every one of us is perfect, or without fault. There are still the gentle sounds of an argument among young ones. There are still complaints about not wanting crust on one's sandwich, or the whining request for more juice. But the ideal is here. The foundation is being taught by example each time we are at the table. The children may have interruptions of trouble, but then we get back to our sweet and happy times of placing that linen napkin on our lap with a sweet smile, and then saying, "*should we say our prayers now?*" This makes the children very happy. We do the good things in the middle of the distractions.

If a home had more formal times of ceremony in daily life, there would be more respect and kindness. Manners have always been known to be a virtue and the foundation of a civilized society. This is why, even though there are mostly little ones at my table, we find joy in a formal approach to tea.

My home is humble and old. My dining table was obtained from a neighbor's front yard with a "free" sign on it, almost 20 years ago. It seats 8. A white tablecloth I use for "best" is more than 2 decades old. My chairs do not match. My dishes are an assortment of mostly gifts and hand-me-downs. Yet, it is so very precious and beautiful to have formal manners and tea time in our very poor family.

It will never be about the money we have, or the quality of the possessions we own. It is about kindness, and morality. It is about virtue, patience, longsuffering, and bringing beauty into our lives by our sweet behavior.

50

Discreet Homemaking

In my childhood home, Dad would sometimes give us little hints on how to keep our home looking nice. He would say, "If you are walking through the living room, and you see paper on the floor, pick it up and throw it in the trash or put it where it belongs. Just do things as you see them, without me having to ask you." This was a habit he practiced in a quiet way throughout his life. He kept his personal things in order and had a beautifully organized garage. He was known for always cleaning up after himself, whether it was sweeping up crumbs on the kitchen floor or tucking in chairs.

Mother was the same way. She would go into the living room and talk to us about our day. If she noticed an empty cup, she would take it to the kitchen and wash it right away. She kept up with the housekeeping as she went along. She never said much to us about how to clean, she was just a quiet example.

Her sister, my Aunt (now in her 80's), was the same way. Her home was always neatly vacuumed and carefully dusted. She was often folding laundry and stacking it neatly before putting it away. She would have hangers nearby for items that needed to go in the closet. Socks were kept together; facecloths were in a neatly folded pile. Everything was lovingly and carefully put in order. She did it all calmly and with a smile as she visited with us.

I call this all "discreet homemaking." It is a way of keeping house which no one really seems to notice. It is doing those little things throughout the day that is not appreciated or acknowledged. It is doing necessary work such as sweeping behind the kitchen trash barrel, putting fresh towels in the bathroom, straightening the couch pillows, and opening the curtains each morning.

It is important to shake out the rugs, sweep the steps, and dust the windowsills. It is lovely when we make all the beds, do the laundry, and straighten the pillows. These little unseen tasks are what make a home look pleasant and comfortable. It is a work that mostly goes unnoticed. But when it is done with a loving cheerfulness, by one who cares, an orderly home is discreetly created in the quiet of the day.

51

Spreading Christmas Cheer

I was in the most beautiful house this morning. It is a historic house in a small city of Vermont, not far from where I live. It is being used as a business with an office for a local professional. Yet, it looks just like a home from a Dickens' novel.

There was a set of double doors to start with. This led us to a small enclosed room and another large door. Soon we were in the entryway. To the left we saw a mirrored rack with a place for umbrellas. Garland and delicate holiday lights were all around. There was a red bench by a window for guests to wait. A large staircase with a beautiful wooden banister was decorated with red bows and garland. All along the wall leading to the upstairs rooms, there were old paintings and historic pictures. Underneath it all, I could see some peeling paint and old finishing. This only added to the charm.

I sat on the bench to wait. Looking off ahead, there was a door ajar letting me see a blazing fire in an old fireplace. I saw a pretty couch and chair with afghans and white lace over them. There were stockings by the fire and an incredible ambiance of a Dickens' Christmas home.

I was in awe of all the time and effort it took to decorate the old house to delight all who entered there. It was absolutely lovely and peaceful!

Back at home, I am listening to Christmas music and doing some baking. I made a white cake for one of my children who has a Christmas birthday. Tomorrow I will be making homemade sugar cookies and fudge. These will be placed in wax paper-lined boxes and given as gifts to my family as they are able to come by to visit, over the next few days.

On Christmas morning, I will be making a special breakfast to share with my grandchildren. In the afternoon, I will serve a nice dinner to delight the family.

This is my small way of spreading Christmas cheer.

52

Teaching Hymns to Papa

During all my years as a mother, the children and I spent time doing family Bible study. We would take turns reading the Bible, sing hymns out of the hymn books, and then close with prayer. Through those years Papa heard our songs and learned some of them. He rarely joined our Bible time because he worked long hours or was very tired.

After his disabling accident three years ago, he was able, and willing, to do daily Bible time with me. We have been reading through the entire Bible. We also sing hymns and pray.

At first, I would select a couple of hymns he already knew. He started to mark the pages so he could easily find them later. Some days I would say, "Let's learn a new hymn tonight." I would sing and he would follow along, joining in as it became familiar.

The other day, I came home from church service, where the congregation had sung "Victory in Jesus." I had forgotten all about that song. That evening, I introduced it to him and he was very happy. It has become one of his favorites. He also loves, "Just a Closer Walk with Thee," and "Trust and Obey."

Sometimes, when Papa is struggling with pain he just listens while I sing, or read the Bible, to him. He has even memorized the page numbers of most of the hymns we know. He can call out any one of them I am looking for. I might say, "What number is 'Softly and Tenderly Jesus is Calling,'" he will call out the number for me. I appreciate this so much and am inspired at how much he loves the old hymns.

Some days, when Papa is puttering around the house doing little projects, I hear the sounds of "Amazing Grace" as he sings quietly while he works.

*We have a set of hymn books called, *"Soul Stirring Songs and Hymns,"* published by Sword of the Lord, copyright 1989.

53

The Little Church Bibles

One Sunday morning, my grown son and I were getting ready to take my 5 –year old grandson and 3 -year old grand-girl to Church with us. I wanted to find a few treasures to keep in my purse so the children would behave. I remembered a couple of little Bibles that are in my home library. I have had them for many years but do not remember where they came from. They are just small New Testament pocket Bibles. One is pink and the other is blue.

When we were in the Church parking lot, I turned around to look at my grandchildren in their car seats. I told them, "I have special Church Bibles for each of you to hold while we are in Church." I picked them up out of my purse to show them. They were so excited. "But you have to be good. You can't cry and you can't whine." I put the Bibles away. They nodded sweetly and agreed to my conditions.

Once we got settled in the pews, the children looked at my purse and waited expectantly for the books they were to hold. I gave grandson the blue book and grand-girl the pink one. I said, "These are the Church Bibles. Be careful with them."

The children sat quietly and reverently for quite some time. They kept the books open and looked through the pages. When it was time to stand up to sing, I handed grandson a hymn book. He shook his head and said, "No, I will use the Church Bible." I smiled at him. He wanted to use it to sing out of, as if he had his very own book for all the church service. It was so precious.

Halfway through the service, the children needed other diversions to sit still. I gave them a pocket calculator, a small pamphlet, and my paper fan. Somehow, we made it through the service without too much noise and fidgeting.

When we got home, I put the little Bibles back in their place. The children felt so honored to have used them. I will bring them each time we get to go to Church together. It is a precious habit for them to enjoy. It will help them learn the beauty and reverence of Bibles and Churches.

54

The Beauty of Mitzvahs in the Home

Mothers ought to have a disposition of benevolence. There is a sweet, peacefulness to joyfully doing good deeds when it is part of one's character.

In Jewish culture, the term for obeying a commandment, or doing a good deed, is called a "mitzvah." When my children were little, they would be so happy when they did something nice, or said their prayers, or willingly shared a toy. They would say with a contended smile, "I am doing mitzvahs!" Or, when they noticed a younger sibling doing kind things for others, they would say, "You just did a mitzvah!" It made them so happy. Why? Because doing this precious work brings you close to the Lord. It creates a bond with our Heavenly Father as we follow out the beautiful Scriptures, which is a lamp for our feet and a light on our pathway.

The more sweet things one does, the more ideas one gets for continually doing good. It also blesses others, encouraging each other in the Lord. Being around others, or reading about and seeing those who are dedicated to Scripture, who are God's own children, will strengthen us. It is like coming in contact with little lights that brighten our own light, guiding us along the path to Heaven.

In the morning, when some of my grandchildren are here for breakfast, they look over at me, while I explain the steps for saying the prayer. I tell them, "First we fold our hands. . ." I wait as eager little ones copy my actions. "Then . . . we bow our heads and close our eyes." I sneak a look to see that they are doing this as well. "Then we say our prayer." At the end of my short prayer, I have them say "Amen" along with me. Their precious smiles are so sweet and they love doing the prayers.

When I take out my hymn book and sing to the children, they learn the beautiful songs that lead to holy living. My daughter tells me that, later on in the day, when the children are off playing by themselves, she can hear them singing, "Bringing in the Sheaves."

It is by doing what we love most that affects the family. If we love holy things, the children will want to follow our example. Oh, how happy is the family when it is full of the blessings of mitzvahs. This is what makes home beautiful!

55

The Pink Bible

A few years ago, when I was in Alabama, we went to a large Christian book store. We don't have anything like it here, so I was delighted to go inside and look around. One of the treasures I found was a small, pink, King James Version of the Bible. It is a bright, dark pink in color with a ribbon marker. This is now my travel Bible.

I use it on trips, and whenever I go to church. It is very new and easy for me to look up passages of Scripture. I would not want to bring my main, house Bible.

When I was a young teenager, my parents gave me an imitation leather- bound King James Bible. My name was inscribed on the front cover. It has my full maiden name. This is the Bible I have used all of my life. It is falling apart. It is in bad shape. I have many sections marked and highlighted from so many years of use. The binding is also very loose and has mostly come apart from the pages, but I am very careful with it here at home. It is my main Bible, my house Bible, which I use for most of my readings.

I am grateful that I can continue to preserve my old Bible by not taking it out with me. The Pink Bible is kept on the hutch in our front parlour. If I have to run out the door for Church, or for an overnight trip, I can easily grab it on my way out the door. It is a treasure.

56

The House Comes First

I have been thinking lately about how empty many neighborhoods are these days. There are all kinds of houses and apartments that are left without a keeper for most of the day. It is hard to imagine driving through a lovely neighborhood, on a weekday, and seeing no children playing, nobody taking laundry off the clothesline, no families on the front porch, and nobody tending the front walkway.

What is causing all these houses to be empty? Could there be a loss of love and appreciation for home?

I love this quote by G.K. Chesterton:

"There are two ways of getting home; and one of them is to stay there. The other is to walk round the whole world till we come back to the same place ..."

Empty homes seem to be the modern way of life for our culture. Babies and children are in daycare and parents are at work. Grandparents do not commonly live with their grown children anymore like they did in the past (particularly in Italian homes). Can you imagine what a help it would be if grandmother lived at home and could help care for the children and tend the house? It would be a blessing to her as well as to the family.

The Christian Home, a godly home, has tremendous value to our well-being. It is to be a restful, pleasant place. It must be cultivated by someone. Someone must be the keeper, the one who "keeps the home fires burning." Someone ought to be home. Mother is the ideal (and Biblically appointed) keeper.

Home can almost be like a hobby. It is where we spend our time decorating, cleaning, dusting, and greeting visitors. It is a place to provide wholesome, nourishing meals, clean laundry, and a comfortable bed in which to sleep. It is a place to rest and spend time with the family. It is a place of security and contentment. There is much to do in order to keep it happy. Some people spend a great deal of time on hobbies. These hobbies are times of entertainment and recreation. If a large portion of that time was spent in the care and love of home, it would be an enjoyable place to be.

We need a priority of home. The House must come first. What we do there each day builds memories we will cling to in later life. Let them be good memories.

Here are some practical ideas to bring life back into our neighborhoods by tending our homes:

1. Arrange your schedule so you can be home more often.

I sometimes see teenagers roaming the streets looking for mischief. I wonder if it is because nobody is there to make a real home for them.

2. Make a list of daily chores and do them.

We are constantly tempted by distractions to do many things. The television, computer, telephone, invitations out, craft projects, and reading are enjoyable but must have their slot of time. The chores have to be completed before we have the fun. (dishes, laundry, sweeping, meal preparation, etc.)

3. Simplify your possessions.

We will always need to sort clutter. Things come in each day and we must discard what is not necessary. It is a tremendous waste of time and energy to have too many things in our house that we do not use or need.

4. Avoid spending money.

The greatest trouble in the home is the lack of careful use of money. In our culture we are constantly tempted to buy, to shop, to spend. Do not yield to this temptation. Do not give in. Learn to spend money carefully and as little as possible. It is better to have money saved "for a rainy day" than to have a financial calamity hit and cause you to fear the loss of a comfortable home.

5. Don't leave home until you make your bed.

I know this sounds simplistic, but the simple act of making your bed will help inspire a clean and orderly home. I do not want to go out on an errand or to an appointment, unless I know I have done my work at home. This starts with making my bed.

6. Evaluate how you are spending your time.

If you are busy with too many outside commitments, this will often cause you to neglect your house. You will be stressed out and anxious. If we do not have the time or energy to maintain a happy, neat home, we must stop all the extra activities that take us away from our main work at home. This will help make us sweet with a gentleness of spirit.

7. Enjoy your labors.

Decorating and cleaning the living room and then sitting down to admire your hard work is a blessing. When you are outside tending the laundry on the clothesline, enjoy the serenity of the fresh air, the retreat - like feeling of doing wholesome work in a lovely setting. Find happiness and joy in the work of keeping the home.

8. Do pretty things.

We ought to present meals in an attractive way. Set the table with silverware, napkins, real dishes, and present the food in pretty serving bowls. This will invite the family to want to come to the table and enjoy eating together. Make the work look pretty. Make the home look pretty. Do your hair nicely and wear a lovely apron. Make home a pretty place.

9. Make it look like a Christian House.

There are paintings and wall art full of Scripture and quotes from great ministers of the past. These types of decorations will inspire you and your guests. At the very least, each Christian home ought to have the 10 commandments posted by the door. (You can type these up directly from Scripture.) We have them there as a rule of life, something that we love and find joy in observing.

10. Keep Love Strong.

A house of forgiveness, mercy, kindness, charity, and love will be a happy home. These are daily acts that must constantly be in service.

11. Keep dust off the Bible.

The foundation of a godly home is the Lord. The Most important part of good housekeeping is daily Bible reading. This ought to be done alone and with the family. It does not have to be formal, but just picking up the Bible and happily reading will bring a great blessing on the home.

This is all "housework" and it is wonderful work that we can enjoy. When home is our priority we find joy in our daily lives. This provides a happy place for our children and families. A great deal of our recreation and entertainment can come just by keeping house. If more mothers could do this at home, wouldn't we have lively, pleasant neighborhoods?

57

Going to Church with Grandmother

This past Sunday morning I went to church with my 3 and 4-year old grandchildren. We were the only ones in the house able to go that day. I was so happy when their Mother offered to let me take them, since I dislike attending services alone.

The children were so sweet and cute. We had a nice talk in the car before we went into the building. I told them we would not cry or whine in church. They sat up straight in their car-seats and said proudly, "We won't cry and we won't whine."

During the service, the children stood when the congregation stood. I handed them each a hymn book and they opened them up, held them on the back of the bench in front of them, and tried to sing along with everyone else.

When it was time for the offering, I pointed out the usher holding a bag. I gave each child a little money and told them to put it in the bag when it came to our row. The usher was an elderly gentleman. He smiled patiently as each little one deposited their offering. The children were so pleased with their efforts.

Halfway through the service, the children started fidgeting. I gave one my pocket calculator and the other a little diary notebook with a ribbon bookmark from my purse. That held their attention for quite awhile so we could all sit and listen to the preacher.

Not long after, we stopped at the store to buy donuts and juice to bring home for the family. It was the promised reward for being good children at church. It was wonderful!

58

Efforts of Holiness

Sometime last year we signed up for cable television. I thought this would be a good idea to keep Papa happy when he is resting. I didn't realize that Dr. Charles Stanley was on every week. So, this has been a great blessing for me. Every Sunday, I have been watching it. Most of the time, I am interrupted by the grandchildren and do not get to see all of the sermons, but every little bit is wonderful.

Soon I learned to program the television to remind me when a Dr. Stanley sermon was about to start. One Saturday night, while I was already in bed sleeping, a notice came up on the television while Papa was watching a movie. He accepted the notice and watched the sermon instead. He told me the next morning. I was delighted.

This got me to thinking. I searched the program guide to see what other preaching was available. I found that old, classic sermons of Billy Graham crusades were on about once a week, very late at night (when I knew Papa would be up watching television). So, I programmed a reminder for these as well. Papa has now gotten into the habit of stopping whatever show he is watching and accepting the notice to watch the old Billy Graham sermons. This is such a blessing to both of us! He tells me about them the next day.

Each evening we have our Bible time. We read the Bible and then sing some hymns out of the hymn books. Papa wears his reading glasses and sits close to the lamp. He suggests "Amazing Grace" or "Sweet by and by." We sing anywhere from one to three hymns and then we close with a prayer. These are precious times.

Each little effort at worship or holy duties brings us closer to the Lord. It makes our spiritual hunger stronger while weakening our worldly interests at the same time. These are small, feeble steps we take to do what is right and good in this dark world. It makes us spiritually strong and gives us great peace and happiness. This is what bonds a family together in joyful Christian fellowship.

59

The Company Ready Home

There is usually a main room where guests first see when they enter a home. This is often a kitchen or living room. These are the common rooms we housekeepers try to keep the neatest. We also do our best to keep the bathroom tidy.

It is not possible to keep all rooms, of a house, perfectly organized and spotless at all times. This is because we do not live inside a magazine cover photograph. Our homes are not going to be "picture perfect." But we do well when we keep the main rooms company ready.

I have often read of the different temporary homes which Caroline Ingalls and her family lived in. She did a few specific things on a daily basis:

1. She always swept the floors each day, even dirt floors in a sod house.

2. The beds were made each day. She made her own and directed her girls to make theirs. This was an expected chore.

3. After each meal, she and the girls would wash and put away the dishes. She would put a clean tablecloth on the table. Then she would put the Kerosene lamp neatly at the center of the table. It

made things look pleasant and tidy.

4. All were expected to sit up straight and use their manners, even if they were camping near the river on their way to a new homestead out west.

There was a time when they didn't have much and the children had been sick with Scarlet Fever. I believe this was in the book, "On the Banks of Plum Creek." Some company was stopping by unexpectedly. Ma (Caroline) worried about what food she could serve, since nothing special was available at the time. Laura, who had been taking care of everyone said something like, "If it is good enough for us, it is good enough for them!" This is so sweet because the way in which they lived, good housekeepers, hard workers, and simple living with dignity, made any meal they served to the family, or to guests, a blessing.

In these modern days, we can certainly take a few minutes throughout the day to keep things neat. I like to polish the bathroom sink, wash mirrors, and put out a fresh towel each day. I also make my bed each morning and open the blinds to let in the cheerful sunshine. I straighten flower arrangements (these are assorted plastic flowers that make things look extra nice all year round), straighten chairs, and put everything "to rights" in the main parlour. This helps to keep our home looking inviting and pleasant.

It is good to just keep the house looking nice in case unexpected guests show up. When my parents were in their elder (retirement) years, they used to do some extra tidying on Sunday afternoons, as that was the common time when church members would stop in to see them once a month or so. Mother would be sure to have some coffee cake on hand for refreshments. She and Dad would dust the furniture and vacuum the carpets. They would make the kitchen counters and table look extra pretty. This was for "just in case" company came. If nobody stopped by that week, they would enjoy the special treat and the extra lovely home regardless.

Years ago, one of my grown daughters used to love to drop in for a surprise visit. She lived a few hours away and I never knew when she would just show up for the night, or for a day- visit. I always wanted to have a warning so I could buy special food I knew she would like. As the years went by, I realized that I would much rather have her just show up unexpectedly. Surely, she would enjoy any food we had on hand because it would be made with love. It was much more fun to have her come by without a warning. She loved to see how happy and surprised I was to see her!

In my childhood home, special treats like cake or popcorn were reserved for once a week or special occasions. Often this was on a weekend. If company happened to stop by, they would share in the refreshments. If they happened to show up on a weekday, they would have the common fare of whatever meal we were having - nothing special. But we made sure our house was always decent and neat so we could share our happy home and life with our guests.

Very often, "Nothing special" in a cared- for, humble home is just what company would love to see.

To have a company ready home just means we housekeepers are doing our job of keeping a decent and tidy home. We look as nice as we can (as representatives of our homes), and gladly welcome weary visitors with a smile and with grace.

60

Holy Living in a Modern World

I have spent many months savoring over the reading of D.L. Moody's biography, which was written by his son in the year 1900. One specific passage has been often on my mind. Preacher Moody traveled significantly in his work. At one point, he was heading home to his family, and stopped his journey to pause for the Sabbath. He spent the Holy Day in a lodging house and rested. We know this because he wrote a letter on that day. It was addressed to members of his church. Part of it is as follows:

"I need not tell you how much I would like to be with you on Fast-day, but God has ordered it otherwise. As I am alone to-day with none but my blessed Master, waiting in this hotel for the Sabbath to pass, so that I can get on to my home. . ." (p.150)

I keep thinking about this, about the amount of dedication he had to actions of holiness in life. He did not just read and preach the word of God, he deliberately followed it.

It seems strange these modern days to stop traveling during the Sabbath – to observe it literally – in such a busy world, where it is not common to acknowledge anything of religious duties. It may seem strange but it is certainly possible.

This is something I will spend my entire life trying to emulate. We constantly forget that there is a Sabbath. We forget basic duties that bring us close to the Lord. We forget to pause and do what will greatly bless us. It is a daily internal battle between ourselves and our modern world.

The "modern world" will always be one of new inventions. It will be one of changing fashions and changing trends. We will always be told to "get with the times" and to stop being "old fashioned" in our living. This kind of "modern" world, the world that is not my home, is always different, in each generation. It is always progressively more corrupt than the last. It is a "live for today" kind of thinking. Yet, those seeking holiness live the unchanging way of the old paths. We live for eternity.

We know we are "Strangers and Pilgrims" on this earth. We are a curious, set   apart lot. We love and adore the narrow way of peace and joy and the beautiful quest for piety. It is a joy to make every effort possible, with great anticipation of happiness, to live holy in our modern world.

61

To Brighten and Beautify Their Lives

Every home ought to have a Mother. She is the light of the family. Her innocence, her happiness, her virtue shines throughout the house. Her presence ought to inspire goodness and kindness in the hearts of the residents.

In an ideal home, Father doesn't bring complaints or trouble from his outside business. His job is left at the welcome mat. In the old days, a good gentleman wouldn't dream of burdening his wife with business troubles for one important reason: He wanted her to remain sweet and unruffled. He needed his wife to be the happiness of home so he could rest and recover from the world. Why would he bring the difficult and painful world (like the mud on his boots) into his cozy, peaceful home?

One sweet way a wife could prevent hearing the troubles of the world, may have been to simply say, "Oh how very sad. It is painful to hear such things." It would be apparent that talking of the cold, hard world brought her sensitive heart almost to tears. No man wanted his wife sad or unhappy. No man wanted his wife hardened and cold. He wanted her peaceful. He needed her joy to keep home a restful place to be. Most men, in the old days, when they proposed marriage, were known to say, "I will do everything I can to make you happy." Or, as I've heard from some others, "I will work hard, even break my back, making you happy." It was clear men wanted a gentle, saint-of-a-wife, an angel, whose happiness would brighten his home.

Men were the protectors of their wives. They protected their happiness and they kept them safe. This world has always been a dangerous place. Grown sons were the bodyguards of their mothers, when on outings, if Father was not there. Men had an instinctive need to keep Mother safe. They guarded the treasure of the home. Men were the providers of their wives and children. They took the burden of earning the living. A woman's nature is to nurture and to be peaceful in the home. When she is taken out of that sphere, earning the living, she becomes hardened. She tires out easily. She is not kept fresh and healthy when she has to take on the stress of the world to earn the bread. Good men did not want that for their wives or for their mothers. In the old days, sons would even support their widowed mothers because they knew her precious place was in the sheltered home.

To keep mother a saint, she was protected at home. When the family were out in the world, they knew mother was home praying for them. They knew she was reading the Bible, singing hymns, and making them nourishing food. The family knew there was a beautiful, heavenly light, shining at home to brighten and beautify their lives.

62

The Privacy of Home Life

I used to walk past historic homes in the suburbs of Boston on my way home as a child. There were large old Estates with beautiful fences and pretty gates to close in the private grounds. The landscapes were lovely in spring and summer months as all the flowers were in bloom. There was such a sense of rest and peace in those properties.

I love houses that are set back away from the road. They are more private and quiet. I also love to see a variety of rooms in a home. There is more peace when you can go from room to room. I see many homes of today with an open feel to them, as one enormous room is designed to hold the kitchen, dining, and living areas. It seems so busy and there seems to be a lack of privacy. If I were able to design a home, I would want a separate dining room, a formal living room, and a separate kitchen. This is a similar style to the home I grew up in. It was my grandmother's house. I would also love a room for a library with large windows to look at the grounds of a humble estate to see wildflowers and hear birds chirping in the trees. I love the peace and respite of a large old home with many rooms. I love the beautiful grounds set away from a busy street. It is a place of privacy and a respite from the busy world.

Home should be a restful retreat where the family and their visitors can have places of comfort and quiet. It would be lovely if cameras were rare and not pulled out to snap photographs every few minutes to share with the world. Home should be a place of privacy.

It used to be that we had to buy film for our cameras. We could only take so many pictures at a time. We reserved them for special occasions like birthdays and holidays, with occasional photographs of daily life. Then we had to wait for the film to be developed before we could share the pictures with others. This was part of keeping things private. Our family photos were shared only with family. We would share only a select few with close friends or guests when they visited. We are losing part of our privacy when we share every aspect of our lives with the public. This is taking away some of our peace and our rest.

Home and family used to be a special thing that we wanted to protect. We wanted to maintain that quiet and that happiness of rest from anxiety, busy-ness, and stress. Home was where Mother and Father were keeping the hearth cozy and the dinner warm in the kitchen. It was a quiet place we felt loved and safe. It was a place of privacy. This was where you could tend the gardens, maintain the homestead, and enjoy the family while shutting out the world for a time.

Even in city apartments there are often a few rooms where you can find peace and rest. There are often window boxes for flowers, and little balconies for plants. Some may even put up a divider wall of a floral sheet, or curtains, to make a little separation when a cozy, quiet spot is needed. One of my grandmothers lived in a tiny trailer, in her later years. She had been a widow for quite some time and was living on the back grounds of her son's property down south. The home was very small, consisting of two rooms and a hallway. The kitchen was in the hallway. It divided the front sitting room from a back bedroom. It was very little but so peaceful and pretty. She made it a restful place.

Whether the home is large or small, when the door of that home is closed, there is a private world for just family and home life. It is a place of peace and quiet from the hectic world.

Oh how nice it would be to cultivate a private home in today's world. We can recreate that old time feel by setting up our rooms and yards in a way that has some separation from the public. This would be such a happy place where one can rest a weary heart from the anxiety of life. This is where one could rest and recover before going back out to do one's necessary work in the world.

63

Setting up a Guest Room

An unexpected visitor was arriving shortly. It was to be for an extended stay. We needed to get a room ready for our guest. Sleeping on a couch and living out of a suitcase was not going to work for someone who needed a temporary *home*. This was to be a place of recovery, and of comfort, for one who was weary from the world.

We have a small back room which used to be a bedroom. It is also a laundry room with a full closet. I was so grateful we had completely emptied the closet over this past winter. The room has a charming window facing the back property. There is a view of the river at the edge of our estate. The window is covered with a white lace curtain, and offers privacy with an old-fashioned shade.

We had to remove a few pieces of furniture, including a full-size bookcase. I had quite a time finding places for all my books. We then removed a couple of chairs and a corner end table to make room for a dresser.

We have a pretty, sage - green dresser which was refinished about 12 years ago by great-grandfather when he and great-grandmother (my parents) lived with us. The dresser belonged to my mother. They were kind enough to leave it here for us when they moved south a few years ago. It has been sitting downstairs for quite some time, waiting for some use. This would be the perfect piece for our makeshift guest room.

Mister found an old mirror we had picked up at a yard sale a few summers ago. The frame needed a little work so he spray-painted it with a pretty silver color; from a can he had leftover in the garage. This spruced - up mirror went on the wall over the dresser.

A twin-size bed was quickly located and brought into the room. I had to purchase an inexpensive set of sheets and a new pillow. A pretty, old lamp sits on the corner of the dresser. I placed an empty picture frame for our guest to put a family photograph inside. This would help make it look comfortable and home-like. The room was freshly vacuumed and looked lovely for our guest.

It is now a quiet, cozy, room for anyone who needs a place of retreat.

64

Tea Napkins

Last month, I found some beautiful Christmas Fabric. I planned to make myself an apron. I have been working on it, little by little, over the last several weeks. I hand-sew because it is easier for me, even if it takes much longer than a sewing machine.

I thought this material was so pretty and cheerful. I wish my local store carried more, but they only had about 2 yards, and then it sold out.

My three -year old granddaughter saw me hand-sewing the lovely material and asked me to make her something with it. I would have loved to make her a little apron, but there just was not enough material. However, there was enough for some tea napkins.

Grandbaby loves Grandmother's napkins. I keep a pretty box of them on a hutch in our front parlour. She helps me set the table for meals, and for tea time. I have plain linen napkins, paper ones, and some homemade ones. Her favorite napkins are pink linen which were a gift from a dear friend. Whenever she reaches for those, I hear her older brother call out to me, "Me'me! She is getting into your tea napkins again!"

I thought she would love a set of miniature napkins for her toy tea set, which is kept here at our house. The Christmas fabric would be lovely for this. There was just enough material to make four little squares. All I had to do was hand-sew the hems around each of them.

I put them in a Christmas tin, along with her plastic tea set. She can use them anytime she likes, and then put it all away in the pretty tin.

I have not finished my apron yet. Baby's tea napkins came first.

65

A Proper Home

I recently watched one of the old Billy Graham crusades on DVD. He spoke on the home. Before his sermon, he called his wife, Ruth, up to the podium to speak. She talked briefly of a Christian home, which was to include regular Scripture reading, prayer, and Church attendance. No matter what trials or troubles were happening in our lives, those three things were the foundation of a Christian home.

This is what I call a "proper home."

There is something called "principle." We ought to live by principle and not by "whims." We ought to live based on duty and not on "impulse." We ought to live by routine and order, and not by "emotions." This will make a home one of security and peacefulness.

So many times, I have been too tired or grumpy to clean the kitchen. If I based my actions on how I felt, I would have a terrible home life. The work we do, based on principle, blesses us tremendously and builds our good character. It cheers us up!

Regular church attendance, family Bible time, and regular daily prayer are the most important works we could ever do to cultivate a proper home. This keeps us close to the Lord. This helps strengthen our morals and our virtues.

Each member of a household is flawed. We make mistakes, we fail, and we do not always do the right thing. But grace, mercy, love, and forgiveness are the acts needed to keep the Christian family together.

A proper home may be a poor one, or it may be wealthy. The means may be bountiful or they may be humble. Yet the parents in that household, who are diligently working for the Master, with great faith and love, will be a beacon of light and holiness. This will bring them great joy.

66

A Lady of Integrity

There are a great many distractions from holy living. Many forms of behavior and recreation seem like harmless fun. But quite a few of them lack old fashioned virtue. It is rare, these days, for us to hear of a person with a good character. This is a person of integrity and moral worth. It can only come from one who has high standards and a set of rules for living, which come from the Bible.

Living a virtuous life, a life seeking holiness through prayer, church attendance, Bible reading, and family worship in the home, is a noble, precious kind of life. It makes one happy as it draws one close in fellowship with the Lord. It is a walking with God, on the path to heaven. Yet, somehow, at the same time, we have our feet in the world. We walk among the beauty of creation but also see the corruption of our sin nature. We have to learn to have standards of conduct to protect ourselves from slipping into vice and bad examples which seek to corrupt us.

One example might simply be the movies. Have you ever been invited to see a modern picture at the theater by some family member you dearly want to spend time with? How easy and how tempting it would be to agree to go just to enjoy the company of someone dear. I have not heard of a new movie which is appropriate for a lady these days. Movies have become more and more ungodly and "trashy" over the years. We have to have standards. One ought to avoid places where inappropriate things are going on. One ought not to see, hear, or go to things that a person of integrity should not be affiliated with. If you are there, then doesn't that mean you approve?

Music on the radio is another example. My father was a man of integrity. When we rode in his car for an outing, he would never have the radio on unless it was a Christian station or some cassette tape of old gospel music. His grandchildren would not dream of asking him to turn on the latest station to hear modern pop or rock music. They knew grandfather was not that kind of person.

We ought to avoid certain books and magazines. For example, if a lady was in the lounge at a hair salon, waiting for an appointment, should she read the latest women's magazine that is put out by Hollywood? Perhaps she could plan in advance to bring her own book or a crossword puzzle to pass the time, while protecting her virtue?

We will always be living in a corrupt world. Times are always going to get worse and worse. The culture is a constantly changing scene. But our values must remain unchanged.

A reputation of moral worth is more valuable than rubies. To be a lady of integrity means we have to learn to decline invitations of worldly activities. This takes practice. It takes discernment. It takes time in the Word, time in prayer, and time spent in peaceful holy duties which bring us great joy.

Our integrity must be based on Biblical standards. This will keep us gentle, gracious, and ladylike. But most of all, most valuable among these traits is humility – being humble and kind. These character qualities are refreshing and rare in this modern world.

67

The Making of a Preacher

Rebecca Stanley found out that her son, Charles, wanted to be a preacher. He felt the call as a teenager. His mother told him that if he was going to be a preacher, he would need a Thompson's Reference Bible. She bought him a copy and gave it to him. Mrs. Stanley loved the Lord and taught this love to her child.

Susanna Wesley was the mother of prolific hymn writer, Charles, and evangelist, John. Both these boys grew up and did incredible things for the Lord. Their mother devoted a great deal of her time teaching her boys how to live a godly life.

There is an old story by Elizabeth Prentiss called, "The Little Preacher." It is about a German family and how the young son, who was very clumsy and a terrible student, became a preacher. In the story, there is a dear, godly grandmother who encouraged this boy in the ways of the Lord.

From what I understand, D. L. Moody had no seminary training. But he had an incredible mother who loved the Lord.

When Billy Graham preached his first sermon, he was 18 years old. An older gentleman volunteered him as a guest preacher. Billy used four borrowed sermons and completed all four of them in 8 minutes! He had no experience and he had to be trained. But his Mother loved the Lord. He said of her, "She gathered us around to listen to Bible stories, to join in family prayers, and to share a sense of the presence of God. She and my father didn't have much education, but my Mother was a woman of God."

We Mothers have a great opportunity to teach our children about the Lord. We do this by living it out before them. God doesn't expect us to be perfect. He doesn't need us to be flawless. He simply needs us to dedicate our lives to Him and to do our very best to do His work. This shines a bright light of holy love and warmth which can quicken the hearts of our children to dedicate their own lives to Him.

As we can see, many great preachers were made in just this way: From humble beginnings with a Mother who loves the Lord.

68

A Covered Bridge

And Graceful Living in Rural Vermont

For the past few weeks, I have been going on little journeys with my oldest daughter and her two small children. These are for necessary appointments and errands. We have been driving through the beautiful rural countryside. The scenery is so peaceful and pretty.

On a recent drive, in a spot where there was virtually no traffic, I asked if she would stop and take a picture of a covered bridge before we drove through. (You can find the photograph on page 65.)

I have been focusing on the beauty of our surroundings, rather than worrying about the housekeeping I need to do back at home. Sometimes I will return home and get right to work on sweeping, laundry, and making things look inviting and comfortable. Since I have been going out so often lately, it is extra tiring. I have to keep reminding myself it is okay to take a nap when I need to, even in the passenger seat of the car on our little drives.

Over the years I have learned to find a way to keep our home neat no matter how busy we are. This does not mean things are always spotless. Everyone makes messes every single day. The neatness has something to do with being graceful and in being a lady. We work hard to keep our dignity and manners. Our homes need similar attention.

Good manners and gracefulness means that we take time throughout the day to tidy up, to cheerfully smile as we make a pretty home out of routine messes. We sweep the kitchen floor a few times a day. We wipe down the kitchen table and counters after each snack or meal. We do the dishes and make the bed before accepting an invitation to go out. We do this because it is good manners and because it what a gracious lady would do.

But this all can get very tiring if Mother does not know how to work in a slow and steady way. She will get stressed and wear out if she does not remember to take precious little breaks. These can be rides in the countryside with the family, or they can be an afternoon rest on the front porch. A little walk in the garden after morning tea is a lovely way to take a break.

A routine of resting after creating beauty in one's home will bring peace and contentment. This is like a bit of culture and quiet to nourish our daily lives.

69

Mending by the Fire

During these cold winter days, it is the ideal time for hand-sewing projects. I will often lay out a few garments on the side of the parlour couch for me to work on. This week, my granddaughter needed her new pajama pants hemmed. They were much too long for her, and I didn't think it would be safe for us to keep rolling them up since she goes up and down the stairs quite a bit. Little ones are always running, and there should be no need to worry about them falling just because we neglect to repair their clothing.

Her pants were thick and warm in pink and white material. I took them up about five inches. I spent part of the early morning hours doing the basic stitches to make sure they were sturdy and secure. When she came upstairs for a breakfast visit that morning, she was delighted to find them. She put them on, smiled, and told us they fit perfectly. I was relieved!

I have sweaters and nightgowns with little rips or loose seams that need just a few stitches to make them well again. The other morning my grandson needed an extra button on his new red -and -blue pajama top. We searched through my sewing box and found a little red one which almost matched the rest. It took just a bit of time to sew it in place while all the children watched.

I have been working on a set of new aprons, but had to put them aside while other sewing needed to be accomplished. There is no need to rush the mending. It is just a part of the home arts. We can do them in a leisurely way as we sit by the fire on our little breaks. It is a peaceful work.

70

Living a Quiet Life

A few weeks ago, I bought three potted geraniums on clearance. One had pretty red flowers. The other two were a gentle pink. The cost was $4.00 for all three. I wanted to brighten up our front garden to add some cheer to our yard. I am often looking out the second story window of our parlour and wanted to see some flowers. This was just what I needed.

It was inevitable that I would neglect them. Once I put them in the homemade garden, I ignored them. I never visited them. I never watered them. I left them alone because I am a terrible gardener.

Despite my failures, the flowers thrived. The red geraniums have constantly kept pretty flowers for me to see. The pink ones look like they will soon produce more flowers very soon. I noticed it just today, when I finally ventured over to see how they were doing. I was delighted.

The sun on the lush green grass somehow makes the property look elegant. It is lovely to walk the grounds and enjoy the sounds of birds and nature. It is a quiet way of life to walk the gardens and see the sights.

I have been settled comfortably here at home. My summer journeys and adventures are coming to a close. It is time to get back to preparations for a rapidly approaching Vermont winter and enjoy the indoors for a season.

I have been cleaning with the help of my little 3-year old granddaughter. She delights in clearing the table and doing little household errands. I will say, "Will you close that door please?" She stands up straighter and says sweetly, as she walks toward the door, "Yes I will." I will ask her to bring me the children's lunch dishes, help me put away puzzles, and make my bed. She is a charming little housekeeper.

Last week we had a wonderful day on the front grounds. There was a birthday for one of the children. There were homemade activities created by the mother of the birthday child. Most of the time, I was holding an 11-month old grandbaby.

There was cake and juice and candy. The games included ring toss, throwing water balloons into buckets, playing with bubbles, and going on the slides. We all had such a lovely time hosted by one of my daughters here at the Estate.

This afternoon, as my lunch guests (grandchildren) were eating, I held the youngest baby and sang "Precious Memories" from the hymn book. It is a lullaby for our life.

Being settled at home, doing all the many duties, and hearing all the noise of family, to me, is quiet. It is peaceful. There is no anxiety from the world's materialism here. There are no advertisements and sales pitches coming at us while we are at the Estate. Home is quiet. It is a quiet life focused on holy living and a happy family.

71

The Little Mother

My afternoon guests are mostly boys along with one sweet, petite girl, Miss Grand-girl. Somehow, despite being surrounded by the rumbling and running of young gentlemen, this 3- year old sister of theirs has many precious, dainty moments.

I give her special homemaking duties. She delights in pouring out the contents of (almost) empty containers into my kitchen sink. Then she carefully puts the items where they belong. (These, of course, would be my little, plastic bottles of ginger-ale.)

She gets the broom and dustpan to help me tidy up crumbs from refreshments the children have enjoyed. The messiest part of the floor is always near the high chair where the youngest infant is still learning to carefully eat his crackers.

The children have bags of plastic blocks, puzzles, play-dough, coloring books, and many other delightful items I keep for them to play with. These are for "upstairs" where Papa and I have our own portion of the house. The children have their own treasures for their section of the "downstairs" where they live.

After the children have been here for quite awhile, there are half-finished coloring pages, baby dolls in miniature rocking chairs, books on the couch, and block houses in - progress all over the parlour floor. Their Mother will call out that it is time to go. The children scramble to help me do some of the cleaning. But usually I finish it after they've gone.

Yesterday, Miss Grand-girl was just about to go back downstairs with the rest of the children, when she paused to say, "Me`me... Don't clean up the babies." She didn't want me to put the dolls away. So, they are sitting in miniature rocking chairs where she can easily find them on her next visit.

The little dear loves my plastic flowers; I have delicate purple ones in pretty vases. I have pink ones in pitchers. There are assorted colors on my sideboard table in different containers. One afternoon, I caught grand-girl taking one of the fake pots of flowers and moving them to another spot. She blushed when she noticed I had seen her. It was time for me to give her a pretty flower of her own.

I went into my dressing room and found a large, light pink one, on a fake stem of green. It is light in material but sturdy. She was delighted that it was for her very own!   "What should we put it in?" was her quiet reflection. She held it in her baby hands and followed me into the kitchen. I had an empty plastic bottle which used to hold chocolate sprinkles. It was perfect for her new flower.

Soon I saw her setting the "potted flower" on the window sill. Then she took one of the baby dolls and put it in her brother's highchair. Next, she moved the flower to a sunny spot on the floor and stood back to admire it. Then she went to see about another doll who needed to sit at the parlour table. She moved the flower here and there and took care of her babies while I watched with a quiet smile. She was decorating and taking care of "children." She was being a precious little Mother.

72

The Angel of the Hearth

How lovely it is to just stay home. There is much productive work to do to keep home happy, clean, and peaceful. I was folding laundry on the parlour couch last evening. I carefully folded linen napkins, washcloths, nightgowns, and towels. These were placed in piles along the back of the couch and all around me. It reminded me of when I was a teenager. I would come home from school, or a walk, and my mother would call out from the kitchen for me to fold the laundry. It was always waiting for me on the couch. I loved to just sit in the quiet of the work and enjoy the labor. No matter what noise was going on around me, whether the television my baby sister was watching, or the sound of my mother's voice on the phone in the next room, I focused on the quiet, peacefulness of the task before me.

There are many things on a housekeeper's mind related to her work. I might be washing the lunch dishes and have to take a break to take the clothes out of the washing machine. I might need to sweep near the baby's highchair or put a fresh tablecloth on the kitchen table. I will lay out a pretty display of fake flowers in a vase, tuck in all the chairs and straighten a pillow in the nearby rocking chair. Then I will get back to my dishes and tidying the kitchen. There are jobs of work and there are jobs of decorating. Both of these are aspects of mission work, which make home a dreamy, happy place.

If I am interrupted by the telephone or a knock on the front door, I can always write what I was doing on a notepad on the side of the refrigerator. This will keep my mind clear and focused on my guest. I can then calmly and peacefully, like a good hostess and housekeeper, get back to my productive work.

I have a hardcover hymnbook on the top of a bookcase, right near my Bible. Sometimes I will crave a song such as "Precious Memories" and take a break to sing while sitting on the couch. This keeps one's thoughts and actions heavenward.

Good manners and kindness, no matter how we feel, go a long way in keeping a cheerful spirit. We will be aggravated by little things, actions and words by those we come into contact with each day. But a polite response with an understanding smile will very often soothe an unpleasant attitude. This is the key to a happy heart – proper manners in all situations.

The more time we spend at home, the more precious time we have to keep a quiet spirit. There will be meekness and gentleness in a soul who is unhurried and not overwhelmed by many outside obligations. The housekeeper who is anchored in heavenly thoughts, prayers, and has a mind set on Scriptural happiness, can take that same spirit of kindness wherever she must go on errands or trips. Her heart must be focused on home and the sweet post in which she is privileged to have. Truly she can set her sights on not just being a Christian homemaker, but on being an angel of the hearth welcoming all who enter her home with a sweet spirit.

Notes:

Unit Three Project:

Set up a Simple Menu Plan

{Photograph on previous page: Mrs. White's Homemade tea napkins for grandbaby's tea set.}

Directions for Setting up a Simple Menu Plan:

The easiest way to set up a weekly menu is by creating a food journal. Each day, for seven days, write down what your family eats at each meal. Once this is finished, you will see what you are habitually making. This might be all you need to plan and prepare your family meals each week.

Sunday

Breakfast

Lunch

Dinner

Monday

Breakfast

Lunch

Dinner

Tuesday

Breakfast

Lunch

Dinner

Wednesday

Breakfast

Lunch

Dinner

Thursday

Breakfast

Lunch

Dinner

Friday

Breakfast

Lunch

Dinner

Saturday

Breakfast

Lunch

Dinner

Unit Three Questions:

1. It is important to have peaceful projects to keep busy and active at home. Are there any sewing or domestic projects you enjoy doing?

2. Small children love fresh baked treats. Are there any special desserts you enjoy making for the family?

3. Tea time is a wonderful experience for learning kindness and good manners. Are there other ways you can model good behavior?

4. What room in your home is your favorite? In what way have you decorated it that makes it special to you and your guests?

Homemaker's Diary

Use this space to write about your experience with homemaking this month. Be sure to share some happy memories of your family.

About the Author

Mrs. White has been married to "Mister" (or "Papa" as the grandchildren call him) for more than 30 years. She is the Granddaughter of a revival preacher; A Beloved Housewife; Mother of 5; and Grandmother of 9. She has been writing on her blog, "The Legacy of Home" since 2009. A retired homeschool teacher, she lives with her family in a humble, old 1850's house in rural Vermont.

For more information, or to find Mrs. White's books, please visit:

The Legacy of Home Press

http://thelegacyofhomepress.blogspot.com

Also see Mrs. White's blog:

http://thelegacyofhome.blogspot.com

Printed in Great Britain
by Amazon

37183498R00116